Sounds Good

On track to listening success

Teacher's Manual 3

PEARSON
Longman

Ken Beatty

Peter Tinkler

Published by
Pearson Longman Asia ELT
20/F Cornwall House
Taikoo Place
979 King's Road
Quarry Bay
Hong Kong

fax: +852 2856 9578
email: pearsonlongman@pearsoned.com.hk
www.pearsonlongman.com

and Associated Companies throughout the world.

First published 2008
Reprinted 2008 (twice)

Produced by Pearson Education Asia Limited, Hong Kong
CTPS/03

ISBN 978-962-00-5895-0

Publisher: Rachel Wilson
Senior Editor: Vessela Gasper
Editors: Jessica Wang, Richard Whitbread, Adrienne Glad
Designers: Junko Funaki, Angel Chan
Illustrators: K Y Chan, Teddy Wong, Roxy Lau, Martina Farrow
Audio production: Full House, NYC
Podcast production: Todd Beuckens, Jose Cruz
Song composition: John Saeki, Nick Walker
Song arrangement: John Saeki, Hisakazu Koya, Richard Whitbread
That's What Friends Are For © Nick Walker (p. 146)

For permission to use copyrighted images, we would like to thank © Max Power/Corbis (p. 22), © STR/epa/Corbis (p. 24, Songkran), © Korea Tourism Organization (p. 24, Chuseok), © Korea Tourism Organization (p. 28, Chuseok), © Lindsay Hebberd/Corbis (p. 28, Onam), © Werner Forman/Corbis (p. 28, Yam Festival), © Macduff Everton/Corbis (p. 34, Shopping Mall), © Gail Mooney/Corbis (p. 34, Parade), © Joel Stettenheim/Corbis (p. 34, Mall Santa), © B.S.P.I./Corbis (p. 36, Neon Signs), © Image Source/Corbis (p. 36, Garbage in River) © Sean Justice/Corbis (p. 48, Woman Making Bed), © Chuck Savage/Corbis (p. 60, Buying Tickets), David Turnley/Corbis (p. 60, Jerry Seinfeld), © Robert Eric/Corbis Sygma (p. 60, Cannes Film Festival), © B. Bird/Zefa/Corbis (p. 60, Magician), © Robbie Jack/Corbis (p. 60, Play), © Howard Pyle/Zefa/Corbis (p. 60, Karaoke), © Pierre Schwartz/Corbis (p. 72, Airplane Seats), © George Hall/Corbis (p. 72, Plane Landing, Plane Taking Off), © Karen Huntt/Corbis (p. 76, Fairmont Hotel), © Mark L Stephenson/Corbis (p. 76, Youth Hostel) © Don Hammond/Design Pics/Corbis (p. 80, Business Traveler), © Sam Diephuis/zefa/Corbis (p. 80, Seatback Table), © Flint/Corbis (p. 118, Man Carrying Boxes), © Erik Freeland/Corbis (p. 120, Website Screenshot), © Walt Disney Pictures/Zuma/Corbis (p. 132, Animation Still) © Paul Seheult/Eye Ubiquitous/Corbis (p. 154, Louvre)

Acknowledgements
We would like to express our gratitude to our Academic Advisors Todd Beuckens, Kaori Nishi, Mee Jee Kim, John Sherman and Sam Shih for taking the time to critically analyze the manuscript and for providing insightful and in-depth comments that were instrumental in developing the listening extracts and activities in this book.

We would also like to thank the many teachers for their useful advice, feedback and support. In particular, we would like to acknowledge Seiko Oguri, Yoshimasa Awaji, Junko Kobayashi, Hiroyo Noguchi, Eunice Izumi Miyashita, Kay Irie, William Fennell, John Alan Smith, Linh Pallos, Toshiki Hara, David Chapman, Carol Duborg, Heebon Park-Finch, Tara Cameron, Laurie Stuart, Kim Sun Young, Choi Woo Hyuk, Zac Sae Jin Kwon, Yi-Mei Wu, Shiuh-Peir Luh, Sue Ou, Sabrina Wu, Nikko Ying-Ying Hsiang, Didi-Ionel Cenuser, Pi-I Chuang, Lili Miao, Doris Lin.

Author acknowledgement
This series is the work of many talented and imaginative people at Pearson Longman, beginning with Publisher Rachel Wilson and Senior Editor Vessela Gasper. Thanks also to countless teachers who gave input. My family—Ann, Nathan and Spencer—is my rock.

Ken Beatty

The publisher's policy is to use **paper manufactured from sustainable forests**

Introduction

Sounds Good is a new listening series designed to help learners of English become effective listeners. The key elements of its instructional design include the following:

Varied listening extracts

Sounds Good offers a variety of listening opportunities including conversations, monologues, radio shows, television broadcasts, lectures, interviews and discussions, all set in real-world contexts. Variety is important not only to give students exposure to different contexts and language registers, but also to arouse curiosity and sustain motivation.

Variety of accents

In addition to American English, the series features a variety of other accents, which expose learners to English as a global language. Exposure to accents other than American increases through the levels, beginning with other native English accents, such as Canadian, British and Australian and progressing to non-native speaker accents from around the world. The communicative value of the different accents is increasing worldwide and tests such as TOEIC© and TOEFL© are following this trend.

Carefully graded tasks

Tasks are carefully graded to ensure that learners receive a lot of language support before listening. The level of difficulty increases progressively throughout the unit and across the levels. This is important for students because it gives them a sense of confidence and achievement.

Clearly stated listening skills

Throughout the series, learners develop a wide range of listening skills including both "bottom-up" skills, such as listening for key words, and "top-down" skills, such as listening for gist or main ideas. The listening skill for each listening activity is explicitly stated on the Student Book page to show the purpose for listening. This is important for learners because it focuses their attention on a particular aspect of the listening situation and is useful for teachers to see at a glance what the focus is.

Pronunciation sections

These sections are specially designed to zone in on key areas of pronunciation that learners of English find difficult. The alternating sections Write what you hear, Learn the sounds and Learn the rhythm use selected words, sentences and short extracts from the main listening tasks to target different areas of pronunciation, with the result of improving students' listening comprehension. Awareness of the sound changes and the patterns of stress and pitch can arm students with strategies to decode natural spoken English.

Speaking opportunities and group work

Each unit provides opportunities for speaking practice in pairs or small groups. The speaking activities are integrated in the unit, and allow learners to personalize the language they have learned, express themselves and discuss their ideas. In working together, students become more active, independent and confident. Listening often occurs in conjunction with reading, writing and speaking and tasks which allow students to integrate these skills provide a richer learning experience and make for more effective listening.

Systematic test preparation

The testing sections are thematically integrated in the units and then revisited in the four review tests. Based on question types used in major national and international tests of English, such as TOEIC©, TOEFL© and IELTS, they help students achieve their wider study goals.

Technology to support independent learning

Learners need more opportunities to listen to English than can be provided through classroom contact. *Sounds Good* uses new media, in the form of podcasts and interactive web pages, to appeal to students to improve their listening skills outside the classroom.

Topic-based, functional syllabus

The *Sounds Good* series is organized around 12 broad themes. Each theme is divided into four topics that build in complexity over the four levels. For example, Unit 10 Theme of occupations, skills and technology is divided into the following topics:

Level 1 Unit 10: focuses on common jobs and the skills that people need to do these jobs.

Level 2 Unit 10: deals with interesting gadgets and inventions.

Level 3 Unit 10: introduces computer technology and software problems.

Level 4 Unit 10: discusses the choices that college graduates face when choosing a career.

Course and class timing

Each *Sounds Good* book provides teaching material that can be completed in one university semester with 90-minute classes or two semesters with 50-minute classes. Here is a breakdown of a typical unit:

Learn the language	10–15 minutes
Listening task one	20–25 minutes
Listening task two	15–20 minutes
Pronunciation	10–15 minutes
Use what you learn	15–20 minutes
Test yourself	15–20 minutes
Go online (getting feedback on student self-study work)	5–10 minutes
Total	90–125 minutes

Note that factors such as class size and student language ability will influence how much time you need to spend on one unit.

In levels 3 and 4 of *Sounds Good*, each unit consists of the following sections:

Preparation

Learn the language

This introduces the unit topic and presents the key vocabulary and functional language. All the words and phrases are drawn directly from the listening extracts in the two listening tasks. On the audio, they are presented first as separate items, then in simple sentences.

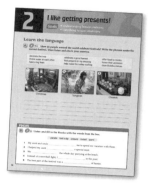

FOCUS This highlights the functional language that students will hear in the listening extracts and use in the speaking activities.

Teaching ideas

Before you begin a unit, find out what students already know about a particular topic. For example, draw a circle on the board and write the word *greetings* in the center. Ask students what other categories and examples they can add. They may come up with *saying hello, introductions, saying goodbye, formal, informal* and so on. Leave this schema map on the board to check later. Students may want to amend or expand on some of their original ideas on the map.

Knowing whether students are already comfortable with the language of a topic will also help you decide if you can move at a faster pace, or whether the students are likely to need a lot more support as you teach the unit.

Once you have had a chance to discuss the topic and have given students the opportunity to share what they know, review the unit goals, asking students what they think each one means. The goals point to the general content of the lessons and can be turned into questions to challenge students: *Do you know how to …*

Pace the lesson for learning. Make sure students are comfortable with everything on this first page of the unit before pressing on; this is the foundation for the unit and students who can understand and use the key vocabulary and functional language are more likely to succeed in the rest of the unit tasks and tests.

Listening

Listening task one

This includes two or three linked listening activities in high-interest contexts, and a structured follow-up speaking activity. The Speak Out activity is designed to place students in situations where they can use the language in the Focus box on the first page of the unit.

The listening skills in most listening tasks are graded to ensure that students move from global understanding of the listening situation to listening for specific details or inference.

Listening task two

This includes three linked listening activities related to Listening task one or the unit topic. In addition to further practicing the vocabulary and functional language introduced in Learn the language, this task introduces some new, high-frequency language related to the topic.

This new language is usually present on the Student Book page either in a word box or integrated in the activity. The new language items are also listed in the Teacher's Manual for teachers who want to pre-teach them before students listen to the extracts.

The Speak out activity is always an integrated skills activity combining listening, writing and speaking. Students practice note-taking skills before they work in pairs to summarize the listening extracts or discuss the topic.

Teaching ideas

Review the listening skills and make sure students understand that they do not always listen in exactly the same way. Sometimes they listen to get a general idea, or to predict what will happen next, or to understand a sequence.

Pause the audio or replay the listening extracts if necessary. Students get more benefit from a lot of listening and will feel more secure with each listening.

Provide enough time for students to check and discuss their answers, and whenever appropriate, give students access to the audio scripts provided on the Teacher's Resource CD-ROM.

When doing the speaking activities, encourage students to use the Learn the language page for support. Circulate around the room, helping students and monitoring their progress.

Pronunciation

Students learning English face significant challenges because they already know and use a different sound pattern. The pronunciation activities in *Sounds Good* are therefore designed to help students improve their "bottom-up" strategies by giving them focused listening and speaking practice in pronunciation features that pose a challenge. Two types of activities target the different areas of pronunciation:

Learn the rhythm

This activity involves patterns of stress and pitch used to express how we think and feel about what we say. Students

practice identifying stress in words, compounds and sentences. For example, stress on country names and nationalities: *Canada* and *Canadian*. They also become sensitive to unstressed syllables which can be particularly difficult to hear. For example, unstressed syllables that are reduced to schwa, such as the first syllable in *Canadian*. Students practice listening to pitch, or changes in pitch, that are referred to as intonation. For example, rising pitch on *Yes/No* questions: *Are you going to do the cooking?* ↗

Write what you hear

This activity focuses on sound changes in connected speech where words join together and sounds are modified or even disappear. The aim

is for students to become aware of some features of pronunciation such as contractions (*I'm*), linking (*I agree, Go on*), assimilation (*cute boy, last year*), deletion (*next day*) and reductions (*Whaddaya*).

Speaking

Use what you learn

This includes two linked speaking activities that allow students to apply their own ideas, opinions and creativity to the unit topic and practice the language they have learned.

In the first activity, students work individually or with a partner to draw simple sketches, complete tables, answer questions or simply think about the topic and brainstorm ideas. The results obtained from the first activity will form the basis for the conversations or discussions in the second activity. It is an interactive activity that encourages students to work in pairs or small groups. Students discuss and personalize the topic, adding their experiences and ideas.

Teaching ideas

Before the second activity, refer students to the conversational cues on the page. Then on the board, write some phrases or additional recycled language that will aid the task.

Always model the conversation with some students first.

During the activity, go around the class, watching and listening to specific pairs or groups. If necessary, take notes to use in the follow-up.

Some groups may finish the tasks earlier or later than other groups. Encourage them to try the activity again for extra practice or simply rearrange the members of different groups to give students more speaking opportunities.

Suggestions for extension activities are provided in the lesson plans of the Teacher's Manual. Use the board to set these up and explain that students can go on to the extension if they are finished with the main activity.

As a follow-up, ask pairs or groups to present their conversations in front of the class.

Alternatively, with the whole class focus on areas of weakness or confusion that you heard while monitoring. Your constructive feedback will enhance students' future motivation.

Testing

Test yourself

This reviews the unit language and includes systematic exam practice based on major international tests of English such as TOEIC©, TOEFL© and IELTS. The Test yourself sections are designed to familiarize students with the test format, instructions and question types. The listening extracts include a variety of recorded texts such as conversations, talks and discussions. The question types are listed in the Scope and sequence for reference.

Review Test

In addition to the Test yourself sections, there are four Review Tests in each Student Book. Each of these tests reviews the topics and the language after every three units. It features the same test formats and question types as the preceding units and includes dictation practice.

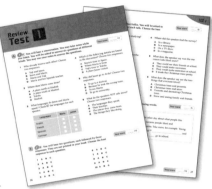

Teaching ideas

Throughout the Teacher's Manual, you will find suggestions for test-taking strategies. Many of these focus on:

- understanding the question type, especially questions where students are asked to find something not mentioned, or are asked to select more than one answer.

- previewing the questions and answer choices before listening in order to quickly recognize the correct answer when it is mentioned on the audio.

- discarding information which is extraneous to the question.

- summarizing information, such as in questions where students need to pick out the main focus of a photo and select the spoken statement that is the best match.

For further testing options, ready-made Unit Quizzes and Semester Tests are available on the Teacher's Resource CD-ROM.

Go online!

The purpose of this section is to provide extra listening. Through the *Sounds Good* website, students have free access to the self-study resources. No registration is required.

Online listening

Found on the sixth page of every unit, this section has been designed for maximum flexibility either in class or outside the class.

In class

It can be used by the teacher as an extra Student Book activity. For this purpose, the audio is included on the Class CDs.

Outside the class

Students can do the activity online via the *Sounds Good* website. Students will find the same activity as on the Student Book page, but in an interactive form. Students click on the audio icon to listen to the extract and then follow instructions such as *click*, *drag* or *type* to complete the activities. Once they are ready, they click on the *submit* button. They will receive instant feedback on their work and have an option to try again, view answers or view the audio script. Note that work cannot be saved.

 ## Podcasts

There are 48 Podcasts in all; one for each unit of the *Sounds Good* series. The Podcast Host introduces these lively shows based around the topic of each unit. These Podcasts are unscripted and authentic, and feature young people from all over the world. Students can download them onto their MP3 players, computers, or mobile phones, with or without the transcript function. Students can also complete a downloadable podcast activity sheet if they (or their teachers) prefer a more focused listening task. Note that the Podcasts are not found on the class CDs.

Teacher's Resource CD-ROM

The CD-ROM contains three useful programs for the busy teacher:

Test Master

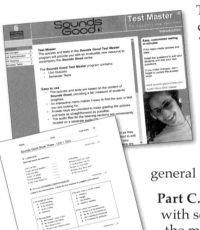

The Test Master contains editable Unit Quizzes and Semester Tests designed to test what students have learned in the *Sounds Good* series. There are 12 short quizzes, one for each unit of the series, and two longer tests, Test 1 for Units 1–6 and Test 2 for Units 7–12. Each quiz and test has three sections:

Part A. Language This part focuses on vocabulary and functional language used in the Learn the language sections.

Part B. Listening Comprehension This part focuses on students' ability to listen to extracts from the Listening task sections and answer general questions about what they hear.

Part C. Dictation In this section, students are given a passage or passages with several words or phrases missing. While listening, students must write the missing words in the blanks provided.

The audio for the Unit Quizzes and Semester Tests can be found on the *Sounds Good* Test Master Audio CD included with the Teacher's Manual.

Audio Script Master

Developed in response to teacher requests, the Audio Script Master provides editable audio scripts of the key listening extracts from the *Sounds Good* series:

- Listening task one
- Listening task two
- Online listening

You can print the audio scripts and use them as they are, or you can edit them to create additional activities to suit your teaching situation or syllabus.

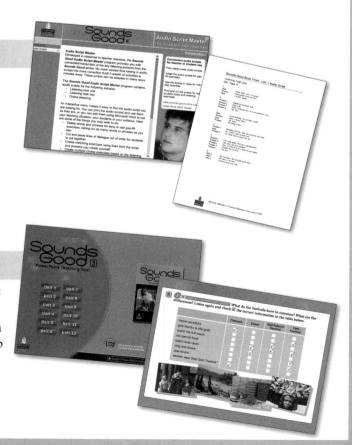

PowerPoint™ Teaching Tool

The PowerPoint™ Teaching Tool includes PowerPoint™ slideshows of the Student Book. Particularly useful for teachers with large classes, the sections of the book can be displayed on a screen at the front of the class to keep students focused on the task. As part of the slideshow, the answers are also provided, which makes checking work easier for the teacher.

Listening skills chart

Throughout the four levels of this series, students will be developing a wide range of listening skills. These skills are marked next to each listening activity in the Student Book. The skills are grouped into four main purposes and this chart explains the meaning of each listening skill.

As students progress through the *Sounds Good* levels, the skills become more challenging: levels 1 and 2 focus mainly on the first two sections of this chart, while levels 3 and 4 include more practice in the last two sections.

Purpose:	Listening for basic comprehension
context	understand the situation, place and time of events
gist	identify the main theme, main meaning or summary
main ideas	identify and understand the most important facts or ideas
key details	identify and understand details that support a main idea
specific information	locate and understand particular information in response to a particular question
key words	identify vocabulary items and work out their meanings

Purpose:	Listening for practical understanding
intention	understand the speaker's plans or desires, explicitly stated
purpose	understand the speaker's reasons for doing or saying something, explicitly stated
feelings	understand the speaker's feelings, explicitly stated
opinions	understand the speaker's opinions on a subject, explicitly stated

Purpose:	Connecting and combining information
sequence	understand the order of events or steps in a process
facts and opinions	distinguish between true information about a subject and what the speaker thinks about this subject
comparison and contrast	identify and understand similarities and differences between things, people and events
cause and effect	understand the causal relationships among events and ideas

Purpose:	Listening for inference
implied intention	understand the speaker's plans or desires to do something, implied through the use of language and manner of speech
implied purpose	understand the speaker's reasons for saying or doing something, implied through the use of language and manner of speech
attitudes	understand the speaker's opinions and feelings, implied through the use of language and manner of speech
predictions	predict the likely developments of an event, topic or idea

Scope and sequence

	Unit	Topic	Goals	Listening extracts
p. 12	**1** Let me introduce myself.	Introductions, nationalities and languages	Identifying countries, nationalities and languages Understanding personal information	Casual introductions Casual conversations
p. 24	**2** I like getting presents!	Festivals in different countries	Understanding festival traditions Identifying festival vocabulary	Casual talks Lectures Casual conversations
p. 36	**3** I can't stand the graffiti.	City and country life, the environment	Identifying the pros and cons of city and country life Understanding environmental issues	Street interviews Casual conversations
p. 48	**4** All the hard chores!	Housework	Identifying chore Understanding duties	Casual conversations
p. 60	**5** Let's do something fun!	Leisure time and activities	Identifying leisure activities Understanding entertainment options	Casual conversations
p. 72	**6** Enjoy your stay.	Travel	Understanding air travel Identifying hotel and travel options	Semi-formal conversations Casual talks
p. 84	**7** Sounds delicious!	International food and table manners	Identifying different types of food Understanding different table manners	Radio interviews Casual talks Casual conversations
p. 96	**8** I'm thinking of getting fit.	Health and fitness	Understanding fitness and diet options Identifying personal workouts and diets	Casual conversations Radio interviews
p. 108	**9** Do you ever wear this?	Fashion and clothing	Identifying clothing and fashions Understanding clothing choices	TV reality show interview Casual conversations
p. 120	**10** Computer Buddies!	Computer technology	Identifying computer technology Understanding telephone helpline information	Voicemail messages Phone conversations Casual talks Casual conversations
p. 132	**11** Seen any good movies?	Movies	Understanding movie reviews Identifying movie terms	TV movie review Casual conversations
p. 144	**12** We stick together.	Friendship	Understanding personal qualities Identifying feelings	Songs Casual conversations
p. 156	**Review Tests 1–4**			
p. 160	**Review tests audio script**			

Listening skills	Pronunciation	Speaking task	Test type
Specific information, Key words, Main ideas, Comparison and contrast	Stress on country names and nationalities	Introduce yourself and others	A question or statement with three response choices not printed in the book
Comparison and contrast, Sequence, Main ideas, Feelings, Cause and effect	Joining final /s/ and /z/ sounds to the next word	Talk about a favorite holiday or festival	A short talk and three questions with four answer choices
Gist, Feelings, Main ideas, Opinions, Sequence, Specific information	Deletion and blending of final /t/ and /d/ sounds with the next word	Talk about preferences: the city and country and discuss the environment	An academic discussion followed by six questions of different kinds
Gist, Specific information, Key details, Sequence, Key words	Rising and falling intonation	Talk about chores	A short conversation and three questions with four answer choices
Gist, Feelings, Specific information, Context, Key details, Implied intention, Attitudes	Contractions and reductions of short words	Talk about leisure activities	A long talk followed by ten questions of different kinds
Context, Cause and effect, Key details, Specific information	Joining final /r/ and /l/ sounds to the next word	Role-play at an airport	Photo description
Attitudes, Comparison and contrast, Key details, Specific information, Key words	Deletion and blending of final /t/ and /d/ sounds with the next word	Describe food types	A question or statement with three response choices not printed in the book
Main ideas, Sequence, Feelings, Key words, Specific information	Strong and weak words in sentences	Talk about health	A short conversation and three questions with four answer choices
Feelings, Sequence, Opinions, Key details, Specific information, Implied intention, Key words	Pronunciation of short words	Discuss fashion	A long talk followed by ten questions of different kinds
Sequence, Key details, Key words, Gist, Implied purpose, Main ideas, Specific information	Pronunciation of short words	Explain how to use computer applications	A lecture followed by six questions of different kinds
Main ideas, Opinions, Feelings, Specific information, Sequence, Key words	Intonation to express attitudes	Talk about movies	An academic discussion followed by six questions of different kinds
Main ideas, Attitudes, Sequence, Specific information, Opinions	Rhyming words	Talk about friendship	A short talk and three questions with four answer choices

Let me introduce myself.

Goals
- Identifying countries, nationalities and languages
- Understanding personal information

Learn the language

A **1** **2** How many countries, nationalities and languages can you name? Complete the table with the words from the box. Then listen and check your answers in the table.

| French | Russian | Spanish | Hindi | Arabic | Australian | Russia |
| Singapore | Spain | German | Indian | Germany | English | Egypt |

	Countries	Nationalities	Languages
A	France	*French*	French
B	*Singapore*	Singaporean	Chinese
C	Australia	*Australian*	*English*
D	*Spain*	Spanish	*Spanish*
E	*Germany*	*German*	German
F	*Egypt*	Egyptian	*Arabic*
G	India	*Indian*	*Hindi*
H	*Russia*	Russian	*Russian*

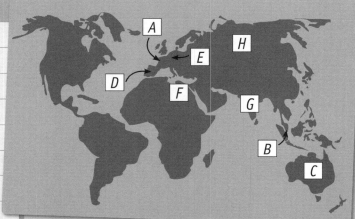

B Now mark the countries on the map, using the letters A–H.

FOCUS

C **1** **3** Listen and fill in the blanks with the words from the box.

great thing   speak   south   introduce   grew up   first language

1 Let me _____*introduce*_____ myself. My name's Tom.
2 I come from the _____*south*_____ of France, near Toulon, but I _____*grew up*_____ in Paris.
3 My parents are from Spain, so I _____*speak*_____ some Spanish. But English is my _____*first language*_____.
4 A _____*great thing*_____ about London is that there are lots of parks.

8

Unit overview

The topic of this unit is introductions, nationalities and languages. In Listening task one, students will listen to six people of different nationalities introducing themselves. In Listening task two, students will listen to some international students introducing themselves and finding out about each other. In the speaking activities, students will have an opportunity to introduce themselves and talk about their hometown and the languages they speak.

Learn the language

- Ask students which countries they have visited or are interested in visiting. Ask students what different languages are spoken in each place. Make a list on the board.

- Have students open the book and look at the world map. Ask them what countries the boxes and arrows are indicating.

- Read the words in the box and ask students to complete the table with the words.

- Allow students a few minutes to finish writing the answers.

- Play the audio (CD1, track 2) and have students check their answers. Tell students that each speaker has an accent depending on where he/she is from. For example, the first speaker comes from France, so she has a French accent. Stop the CD and play each sentence again as often as necessary.

- Review the answers with students. Read through the items in the table (A–H) and ask students for the words in the blank spaces. Tell students that there may be other possible answers for languages as more than one language is spoken in countries like Singapore and India.

Audio script [CD1, track 2]

1   France. I'm from France.
2   French. I'm French and I speak French.
3   Singapore. I'm from Singapore.
4   Singaporean. I'm Singaporean and I speak Chinese.
5   Australia. I'm from Australia.
6   Australian. I'm Australian and I speak English.
7   Spain. I'm from Spain.
8   Spanish. I'm Spanish and I speak Spanish.
9   Germany. I'm from Germany.
10 German. I'm German and I speak German.
11 Egypt. I'm from Egypt.
12 Arabic. I'm Egyptian and I speak Arabic.

13 India. I'm from India.
14 Hindi. I'm Indian and I speak Hindi.
15 Russia. I'm from Russia.
16 Russian. I'm Russian and I speak Russian.

- Have students mark the countries (A–H) on the map.

- Review the answers with students.

C

- Have students read through the words in the box and the sentences to get an idea of what they will be listening for. Tell students that the man saying the first extract has a British accent and the woman saying the second extract has a French accent.

- Play the audio (CD1, track 3) and have students fill in the missing words.

- Review the answers with students by playing the audio again.

- Have students role-play the sentences in the *Focus* box as if they were introducing themselves.

Language note

We usually add an ending (-*ese* or -*ian*/-*iean*/-*an*) to a word for country to change it into a word for nationality. For example, Canada + *ian* ➔ Canadian, Japan + *ese* ➔ Japanese. However, there are also some exceptions, in which no ending is added, e.g., the nationality word for *France* is *French*.

The phrase *grew up in* is another way of saying where you are from. For example, *I grew up in Vancouver.*

Audio script [CD1, track 3]

1   Let me introduce myself. My name's Tom.
2   I come from the south of France, near Toulon, but I grew up in Paris.
3   My parents are from Spain, so I speak some Spanish. But English is my first language.
4   A great thing about London is that there are lots of parks.

1 Let me introduce myself.

Listening task one

A **1** **4-9** Listen for specific information **Six people are introducing themselves. Listen, and draw lines to connect the people to the places they are from and check ☑ the languages that they speak.**

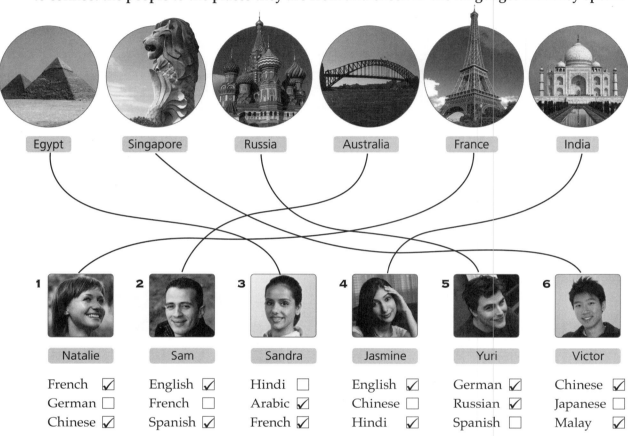

| Egypt | Singapore | Russia | Australia | France | India |

| **1** Natalie | **2** Sam | **3** Sandra | **4** Jasmine | **5** Yuri | **6** Victor |

French ☑	English ☑	Hindi ☐	English ☑	German ☑	Chinese ☑
German ☐	French ☐	Arabic ☑	Chinese ☐	Russian ☑	Japanese ☐
Chinese ☑	Spanish ☑	French ☑	Hindi ☑	Spanish ☐	Malay ☑

B **1** **4-9** Listen for key words **What are the things they mention about their countries and cities? Listen again and write them down.**

1 **Natalie** You've probably heard about the big _____*movie festival*_____ we have every year.

2 **Sam** There are _____*amazing beaches*_____.

3 **Sandra** There are lots of _____*clubs*_____ that play live music.

4 **Jasmine** There are lots of places to _____*hang out*_____.

5 **Yuri** All frozen ponds and rivers become _____*skating rinks in winter*_____.

6 **Victor** It's small, _____*clean and very comfortable*_____.

Speak out!

Work with a partner. Choose two of the above people. Talk about where they come from, the languages they speak and something special about the place they are from.

Use the language in **FOCUS** to help you, but change 'I' to 'he' or 'she'.

9

Listening task one

- Put the class into teams and have them race against each other to be the first team to name all the country icons correctly: Egypt – the Pyramids of Giza; Singapore – the Merlion; Russia – Saint Basil's Cathedral; Australia – Sydney Harbour Bridge; France – the Eiffel Tower; India – the Taj Mahal.

- Allow students to go over the languages on the page.

- Play the audio (CD1, tracks 4–9) and have students connect the people to the places and check the languages they speak. Tell students that Natalie in the first talk has a French accent, Sam in the second talk has an Australian accent, Sandra in the third talk has an Egyptian accent, Jasmine in the fourth talk has an Indian accent, Yuri in the fifth talk has a Russian accent and Victor in the sixth talk has a Chinese accent.

- Review the answers with students.

- Ask students which person sounds most interesting and why.

Audio script [CD1, tracks 4–9]

1
Natalie Let me introduce myself. I'm Natalie Dubois and I'm French. Uh, I come from the south of France, near Cannes. You've probably heard about the big movie festival we have every year. French is my first language, of course, but I lived in Taiwan when I was a child so I speak some Chinese as well.

2
Sam OK, I'm Sam Garcia. I grew up in a small town on the east coast of Australia. My parents are from Spain so I speak some Spanish. The best thing about Australia is that there are amazing beaches.

3
Sandra My name is Sandra Nasser and I'm Egyptian. I speak Arabic and French. I grew up in Cairo, in Egypt. A great thing about Cairo is that there are lots of clubs that play live music.

4
Jasmine Hi, everyone. My name is Jasmine Patel and I'm from Delhi, in the north of India, and I speak Hindi. My hometown is great for young people. There are lots of places to hang out.

5
Yuri My name is Yuri Denisovich and I was born in Moscow, in Russia. Russian is my first language, but I also speak some German and French. A great thing about Russia is that all frozen ponds and rivers become skating rinks in winter.

6
Victor I'm Victor Tam and I'm from Singapore. Like many Singaporeans, I speak Chinese, English, Malay and even some Hindi. A good thing about Singapore? Well, it's small, clean and very comfortable.

B

- While introducing themselves, these people also mention something interesting about the place they are from. Ask students to listen again for what is interesting about each person's place.

- Play the audio (CD1, tracks 4–9) again and have students complete the sentences.

- Ask questions to review the answers with students, e.g., *What's interesting about Natalie's place?*

Speak out!

- Review the language in the *Focus* box on the previous Student Book page.

- Put students into pairs and explain the speaking activity.

- Encourage students to add other details they may know about each person's city or country.

- Note that students are not expected or encouraged to repeat the conversations word-for-word.

Model conversation

A Let me introduce Sam.
B Where's he from?
A He grew up in a small town on the east coast of Australia.
B What languages does he speak?
A He speaks English. His parents are from Spain so he speaks some Spanish, too.

Unit 1

Listening task two

A **1** **10-13** Listen for main ideas) Some people are talking. Listen and circle T for True or F for False.

A Most of the people know each other well. T (F)

B All the people are pen pals. T (F)

C The speakers are from different countries. (T) F

D The speakers are probably all students. (T) F

B **1** **10-13** Listen for key words) Listen again and complete the sentences. Use some of these countries and nationalities to help you.

Chile Chilean Greece Greek the Philippines Filipino Brazil Brazilian Germany German

1 **Carl** Did you say you were from _____the Philippines_____?

Olivia Yeah, that's right. And you're from?

Carl _____Germany_____. I guess we're both a _____long way from_____ home.

Olivia Oh, you're _____German_____? I had a pen pal from Germany when I was in high school.

2 **Dimitris** Hi, _____do you mind_____ if we join you? We're both from _____Greece_____.

Carl What _____part of the country_____ are you from?

3 **Maria** And you're from _____Germany_____? _____Whereabouts_____? Berlin?

4 **Carl** You're from _____Chile_____, aren't you?

Miguel That's right, I'm _____Chilean_____. But I'm not the only South American here. He's one of the students from _____Brazil_____.

Olivia One of them? How many are there?

Miguel Three _____Brazilians_____.

Speak out! **1** **10-13** Work with a partner. Listen again and write short notes about each speaker. Tell your partner what you learn about each one.

10

Listening task two

- The new language introduced in this section includes the following words, phrases and sentences:

Chile	the Philippines
Chilean	Filipino
Greece	South American
Greek	a long way from home
Brazil	pen pal
Brazilian	we kind of lost touch
German	do you mind if we join you?
Germany	Whereabouts?

- Ask students whether they have friends from different countries. What countries are they from?

- Explain that students will listen to conversations among a group of people. Tell students that in Conversation 1 Carl has a German accent and Olivia has a Philippine accent, in Conversations 2 and 3 Dimitris and Maria both have Greek accents, and in Conversation 4 Miguel has a Chilean accent.

- Have students read through the statements quickly.

- Play the audio (CD1, tracks 10–13) and have students circle T or F.

- Review the answers with students. Have students call out words or phrases they heard that helped them decide.

Audio script [CD1, tracks 10–13]

1

Carl	Hi. How's it going?
Olivia	Great. How about you?
Carl	Good. Um, did you say you were from the Philippines?
Olivia	Yeah, that's right. And you're from?
Carl	Germany. I guess we're both a long way from home.
Olivia	Oh, you're German? I had a pen pal from Germany when I was in high school. But we kind of lost touch …

2

Dimitris	Hi, do you mind if we join you?
Carl	No, not at all.
Olivia	Please do. I'm Olivia and this is …
Carl	Carl. My name's Carl. And you are?
Dimitris	I'm Dimitris and this is my friend Maria. We're both from Greece.
Olivia	Ah, Greece! I'd love to go there.
Carl	I was in Athens last year and loved it. The food was great and the people were friendly. What part of the country are you from?

Maria	Dimitris is from Athens and I'm from Larisa.

3

Maria	And you're from Germany?
Carl	That's right.
Maria	Whereabouts? Berlin?
Carl	No, I'm from Garmisch. It's a small town, but a great place to go skiing. In winter, we just walk out our front doors and go for it.
Maria	Sounds great.

4

Miguel	Hi, Carl. What are you guys talking about?
Carl	Oh, hi Miguel. We're just saying where we each come from. You're from Chile, aren't you?
Miguel	That's right, I'm Chilean. But I'm not the only South American here. Hey, Tiberio … oh, he's busy. Anyway, that's Tiberio. He's one of the students from Brazil.
Olivia	One of them? How many are there?
Miguel	Three. Three Brazilians. Oh, I think class is starting again.

- Have students go over the words in the box and the sentences quickly.

- Play the audio (CD1, tracks 10–13) again and have students fill in the missing words.

- Review the answers with students. If necessary, play the audio again.

Speak out!

- The aim of this section is to integrate listening with other skills. In this case, students practice note-taking before doing verbal summaries.

- Put students into pairs and explain the speaking activity.

- Play the audio (CD1, tracks 10–13) once more and have students write notes about each speaker.

- Have students work in pairs to tell each other what they learn about the speakers. Encourage students to share as much information about each speaker as possible, as it they were exchanging information about these people after a party.

Model conversation

A What did you learn about Carl?
B Well, he's from Germany.
A What part of the country is he from?
B I'm not sure. Was it Berlin?
A No, I think he said he's from Garmisch.

1

Learn the rhythm

A **1** **14** Can you hear the difference in stress in the words *Canada* and *Canadian*? *Canada* is stressed on the first syllable while *Canadian* is stressed on the second. Listen to the word pairs and underline the syllables with the strongest stress.

Example: Ko/re/a   Ko/re/an   (same)
                  Ca/na/da   Ca/na/di/an   (different)

1	Eng/land	Eng/lish		**6**	Chi/na	Chi/nese
2	Ja/pan	Ja/pa/nese		**7**	Bra/zil	Bra/zil/ian
3	Rus/sia	Rus/sian		**8**	Sin/ga/pore	Sin/ga/por/ean
4	E/gypt	E/gyp/tian		**9**	Phi/lip/pines	Fi/li/pi/no
5	Ma/lay/sia	Ma/lay/si/an		**10**	Ger/ma/ny	Ger/man

B **1** **14** Now listen again and repeat. Try stressing the correct syllables.

Use what you learn

A How would you introduce yourself? Complete the following sentences.

I'm from _____Xi'an in China_____.
I speak _____Chinese and English_____.
A great thing about my hometown is that _you can see the terracotta warriors and horses from_
over two thousand years ago.

Answers may vary.

B Work in groups of three. Introduce yourself and let your group members ask you questions about your hometown and the languages you speak. Take turns.

A You're from Seoul, aren't you?
B No, I'm not. I'm from Daegu.
C What do you like about your hometown?
B There are lots of places to hang out.
A What languages do you speak?
B I speak Korean and some English.

11

Learn the rhythm

Aim

The aim of this section is for students to identify the syllable with main stress on country names and nationalities and practice their pronunciation.

A word, such as a country name or a nationality, has only one syllable with main stress. The syllable is said louder and longer than all the other syllables in the word. Sometimes a second syllable in a long word has stress. It is called secondary stress and is not as strong as main stress:

ˌJa/pa/ˈnese   ˌsecondary stress, ˈ**main stress**

We usually add one of several different endings to change a country name into the name of its nationality, e.g.,

Canada+ian   ➔   Canadian

However, there are some exceptions, e.g.,

France   ➔   French

Ending	Position of main stress	Example
- ese	on the ending	ˈChi/na Chi/ˈnese
- ian/ -ean/ -an	on the syllable before the ending	ˈE/gypt E/ˈgyp/tian

- Introduce the topic of main stress on country names and nationalities.

- Point out the example. Ask students to compare the pronunciations of the country names and nationalities. What do they notice? Main stress is the same on *Korea* and *Korean*, but it is different on *Canada* and *Canadian*.

- Play the audio (CD1, track 14) and have students underline the syllable with main stress.

- Have students write their answers on the board. Play the audio again to review answers. Ask students to point out any changes in the position of main stress.

- Encourage students to correct any of their mistakes.

Audio script [CD1, track 14]

Example: Korea Korean   Canada Canadian

1	England	English
2	Japan	Japanese
3	Russia	Russian
4	Egypt	Egyptian
5	Malaysia	Malaysian
6	China	Chinese
7	Brazil	Brazilian
8	Singapore	Singaporean
9	Philippines	Filipino
10	Germany	German

- Play the audio (CD1, track 14) and have students listen and repeat the country names and nationalities.

- Monitor and provide feedback on their pronunciation modeling the correct answer if necessary.

Extension

Put students into two teams, and have them use a world map to make a list of 10 to 15 countries, with each team selecting a hemisphere. Encourage students to challenge the opposing team to give the correct nationality for each country name, indicating the syllable with main stress.

Use what you learn

Aim

The aim of this section is to give students the opportunity to introduce themselves and talk about their hometown and the languages they speak.

- Review the unit vocabulary and functional language.

- Have students work individually to complete the sentences.

- Explain the activity and model the sentences at the bottom of the page with two students.

- Put students into groups of three and have them work together to complete the activity. Encourage groups to say something interesting about their hometowns.

- Move around, monitoring the groups and facilitating where necessary.

- Follow up with the class on any points you heard and would like to highlight.

Extension

Ask students to survey each other and make a list of the good things about their hometown. Have groups introduce their hometown to the class.

Model conversation

A There are quite a few good things about our hometown.

B The best thing is the amazing skyline at night.

Unit **1**

Your score:

_____ /10

Test yourself

1 **15** You will hear a question or statement followed by three responses. They are not printed in your book. Choose the best response to each question or statement. Here is an example:

You will hear:

Man   Do you mind if we join you?

You will also hear:

Woman   **A** No, I'm not.
            B No, not at all.
            C That's right.

The best response to the question "Do you mind if we join you?" is choice B, "No, not at all.", so you should circle B.

1 **16** Now listen to ten questions and statements, each followed by three responses. Choose the best response to each question or statement.

1 (A) B   C   6   A (B) C

2   A (B) C   7   A (B) C

3 (A) B   C   8   A   B (C)

4   A (B) C   9   A (B) C

5   A   B (C)   10 (A) B   C

Test yourself

Aim

The aim of this section is to provide exam practice. Students will listen to some questions and statements and choose the best response to each question or statement from three response choices.

Explain the test format. Students will have seven seconds after each question to choose the best response. Neither the questions and statements nor the response choices are printed in the book, so students should focus on the question or statement and predict a possible response.

Play the example (CD1, track 15). Explain that the question requires a response that includes a positive or negative answer. Students should be able to predict a possible response to the question and then choose the response which can best match their prediction.

Point out that the woman saying the responses in Question 1 has a Spanish accent, the woman saying the statement in Question 2 has an Egyptian accent, the man saying the responses in Question 3 has a German accent, the woman saying the responses in Question 7 has a French accent, and the man saying the statement in Question 10 has a Canadian accent.

Audio script [CD1, track 15]

Man   Do you mind if we join you?
A   No, I'm not.
B   No, not at all.
C   That's right.

[CD1, track 16]

1   Did you say you're from Spain?
  A   That's right, the north of Spain.
  B   No, I'm from the south of Spain.
  C   Yes, I'm from England.

2   My friend and I are both from Egypt.
  A   Oh, you're German.
  B   I'd love to go there.
  C   It's a great place for skating.

3   Where do you come from?
  A   I come from Germany.
  B   I don't come from Germany.
  C   I didn't grow up in Germany.

4   How many Japanese students are there?
  A   There are five Chinese students.
  B   There are three students from Japan.
  C   There is one student who grew up in New York.

5   You're from South America, aren't you?
  A   My name is George.
  B   Let me introduce myself.
  C   No, I'm not.

6   What's something you like about New York?
  A   I don't like the noise.
  B   I like the different restaurants.
  C   New York is in the United States.

7   Where are you from?
  A   I'm not from South America.
  B   I'm from France, but I grew up in Spain.
  C   I'm from the university.

8   What languages do you speak?
  A   No, I don't speak Japanese.
  B   My parents are from Russia, but I don't speak Russian.
  C   English is my first language, but I also speak some French and Chinese.

9   What part of the country are you from?
  A   I'm from Germany.
  B   I'm from a small town in the south.
  C   I grew up in Italy.

10   A great thing about Canada is that in winter you can go ice-skating outside.
  A   Sounds great, but I can't skate.
  B   Sounds good, but I can't ski.
  C   Yes, Canada is a big country.

Go online!

Visit the *Sounds Good* website at ***www.sounds-good-online.com***
Click on **Go online!** for extra listening practice.

Online listening

 A **1** 17 Listen for comparison and contrast **Roger and Sophie are talking at a party. What do they have in common? Listen and check ☑ the boxes.**

Sophie …	Roger …	
✓	✓	knows Jack.
✓	✓	goes to university.
✓	✓	was born in another country.
✓	✓	grew up in another country.
✓		speaks French.
	✓	speaks Japanese.
	✓	speaks Arabic.
✓	✓	is going to be a doctor.

B **1** 18 Listen for specific information **Roger may not have told the truth about himself. Listen to Jack and Sophie talking and circle T for True or F for False.**

1 Roger was born in Boston. (T) F
2 Roger speaks Arabic. T (F)
3 Roger speaks some Japanese. (T) F
4 Roger works at a restaurant. (T) F
5 Roger is a chef. T (F)

 Download *Sounds Good* Podcast 25

Now listen to Podcast 25. You can do the activities, read the transcript, or simpy enjoy listening to young people from around the world.

13

Go online!

Students can visit the *Sounds Good* website at *www.sounds-good-online.com* and click on *Go online!* for extra listening practice based on the unit topic.

Online listening

This section can be used in two ways.

Students can use this for some optional, self-study listening practice outside the classroom. Students will see the same activity as printed in their Student Book and they will be able to complete it online, with immediate feedback on their answer choices.

Alternatively, you can use this section in class as an extension activity. The Online listening is recorded on the Class CDs for this purpose.

Students will listen to a conversation between Roger and Sophie in the first part. Roger tries to impress Sophie by telling her some great things about himself. In the second part, Jack, their mutual friend, joins the conversation and Roger nervously disappears. Sophie has a British accent.

Audio script [CD1, track 17]

Roger	Great party!
Sophie	Oh, hi. Oh, yes. It is a great party.
Roger	Let me introduce myself. My name's Roger.
Sophie	Hello, Roger. I'm Sophie. Mm … you're a friend of Jack's?
Roger	That's right. And you?
Sophie	Just met Jack at university. I moved here last week.
Roger	Oh, where do you come from?
Sophie	I come from the north of India, near Darjeeling, but I grew up in England. I moved to Boston to go to university. And you?
Roger	Me? Uh, I was born in … France, in the south of France near Cannes. But I grew up in … Japan.
Sophie	Really, that's so interesting! So you speak Japanese?
Roger	Oh, yeah. Japanese and … do you speak French?
Sophie	Yes, I studied all through secondary school.
Roger	Well, I don't speak French, but I do speak Arabic.
Sophie	That's great! And you're going to university too?
Roger	Mm … I go to Harvard. I'm going to be a doctor.
Sophie	Me too!
Roger	Hey, listen. Let's go out for dinner tomorrow night. Maybe we could get a chance to—

Sophie	Oh, look! Here comes Jack.
Roger	Uh, I … let me get us some drinks. Back in a minute.

[CD1, track 18]

Sophie	Hi, Jack.
Jack	Hi, Sophie. I see you met Roger. Nice guy.
Sophie	Yes, and so interesting. Did you know he was born in France?
Jack	France?! No, he wasn't. He was born here, in Boston.
Sophie	But he said he grew up in Japan. And he speaks Japanese … and Arabic!
Jack	I'm sure he doesn't speak Arabic and as for Japanese, he knows some because he's a waiter at a Japanese restaurant.
Sophie	He doesn't go to Harvard? He's not going to be a doctor?
Jack	(laughs)

 Podcast 25

Encourage students to download Podcast 25. Inspired by the unit topic, it is authentic and high-interest, and features young people from around the world.

2

I like getting presents!

Goals
• Understanding festival traditions
• Identifying festival vocabulary

Learn the language

A **1** 19-21 How do people around the world celebrate festivals? Write the phrases under the correct festival. Then listen and check your answers.

decorate the tree	celebrate a good harvest	offer food to monks
throw water at each other	find presents in my stocking	honor their ancestors
have a big feast	help make the turkey stuffing	clean Buddha statues

Christmas

Songkran

Chuseok

decorate the tree	*throw water at each other*	*celebrate a good harvest*
help make the turkey stuffing	*clean Buddha statues*	*have a big feast*
find presents in my stocking	*offer food to monks*	*honor their ancestors*

FOCUS

B **1** 22 Listen and fill in the blanks with the words from the box.

parade   had a dip   prepare   invited   spent

1 My aunt and uncle _____*invited*_____ me to spend my vacation with them.

2 I helped my aunt _____*prepare*_____ a special meal.

3 We _____*spent*_____ the whole day partying at the beach.

4 Instead of a snowball fight, I _____*had a dip*_____ in the pool.

5 The best part of the festival was a _____*parade*_____ of Santas.

14

Unit overview

The topic of this unit is festivals in different countries. In Listening task one, students will listen to two people telling stories about festivals they have attended: a woman who spent Christmas in Australia and a man who visited Thailand during the water festival. In Listening task two, students will listen to a talk about harvest festivals around the world. In the speaking activities, students will have an opportunity to talk about their favorite holiday or festival.

Learn the language

- Ask students about a recent festival either just passed or coming up. How do they celebrate it?
- Have students open the book and look at the pictures. Ask them what each picture shows.
- Read the phrases in the box and ask students to match them to the pictures.
- Allow students a few minutes to finish writing the answers.
- Play the audio (CD1, tracks 19–21) and have students check their answers. Stop the CD and play each sentence again as often as necessary.
- Ask questions to review the answers with students. For example, *What do people do to celebrate Christmas?*

Culture note

Christmas is celebrated in Western countries.

Songkran is celebrated in Thailand.

Chuseok is celebrated in Korea.

Audio script [CD1, tracks 19–21]

1

Man	I decorate the Christmas tree. I help my dad make the turkey stuffing. On Christmas Day, I find presents in my stocking.

2

Woman	Songkran is known as the Water Festival. People throw water at each other. They clean Buddha statues and offer food to monks.

3

Woman	People celebrate a good harvest, and there is always a big feast. People honor their ancestors during this festival.

B

- Tell students a festival story which is similar to the one in the *Focus* box.
- Have students read through the words in the box and the sentences to get an idea of what they will be listening for.
- Play the audio (CD1, track 22) and have students fill in the missing words.
- Review the answers by playing the audio again.
- Have students role-play a story with the sentences in the *Focus* box.

Audio script [CD1, track 22]

1	My aunt and uncle invited me to spend my vacation with them.
2	I helped my aunt prepare a special meal.
3	We spent the whole day partying at the beach.
4	Instead of a snowball fight, I had a dip in the pool.
5	The best part of the festival was a parade of Santas.

Listening task one

 1 23-24 [Listen for sequence] Two people are telling stories about festivals. How did they celebrate? Listen and put the pictures in the correct order.

1
 4
 2
 3
 1

2
 3
 2
 4
 1

B **1** 23-24 [Listen for comparison and contrast] What do their stories have in common? What are the differences? Listen again and check ☑ the similarities and differences.

		Similar	Different
1	They spent the day outside.	✓	
2	They went for a swim.		✓
3	The weather was hot.	✓	
4	Eating was part of the festival.	✓	
5	They saw a parade.		✓

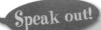

Work with a partner. Choose one of the stories above. Tell it to your partner.

Use the expressions in **Learn the language** to help you.

15

Listening task one

- Tell students that they will listen to two people telling stories about festivals they have celebrated. The woman telling the first story on track 23 has a British accent.

- Have students look at the pictures and say what the people are doing in each picture.

- Play the audio (CD1, tracks 23–24) and have students number the pictures in the correct order.

- Review the answers with students.

- Ask students what else they think the people would do during the festivals.

Audio script [CD1, tracks 23–24]

1

Woman When my cousin in Australia invited me to spend Christmas with her, I hesitated. Christmas in Australia, in the heat of the summer? I always spend Christmas in England with my family. On Christmas Eve, I usually help my mum prepare the turkey stuffing and wrap presents for my brothers and sisters. And then on Christmas Day, I wake up early in the morning to find my stocking filled with presents. But then I thought, I'm not a child any more. I want to try something different this year. And I wasn't disappointed.
Sydney was amazing! On Christmas Day, I woke up to birds singing outside my window, and I spent the whole day partying at the beach, wearing shorts and a T-shirt. We had barbecued seafood, different salads and lots of ice cream. The food was great! Instead of a snowball fight, I had a dip in the sea. There was no snow, no reindeer or a sleigh, but there was a Santa who arrived at the beach riding on a surfboard! I had a great time in Sydney! Next year, I'm going to spend Christmas in Miami!

2

Man Have you ever heard of Songkran? I hadn't. I was traveling through Southeast Asia and ended up in Chiang Mai in Thailand one night in April. The next morning, I went out of my hotel and was immediately shot at with water guns by three laughing kids. At the hotel the manager laughed too, and explained that it was Songkran, the Buddhist New Year

festival, also known as the Water Festival. It was all about getting wet—and getting other people wet, as Thais believe that water will wash away all the bad luck! So the manager gave me a bucket of cold water, and I headed out onto the street to enjoy the fun. I spent the rest of the day wandering through the town throwing water at people. I got soaking wet myself, but it was very refreshing in the heat of Chiang Mai! The next day, I watched some of the ceremonies, such as cleaning Buddha statues and offering food to monks. I was also invited to a feast, but the best part was a parade of ladies on bicycles, carrying beautiful umbrellas.

- Put students into pairs and have them go through the sentences in the table and discuss the similarities and differences between the two stories.

- Play the audio (CD1, tracks 23–24) again and have students check the similarities and differences.

- Review the answers with students. If necessary, play the audio again.

Speak out!

- Review the expressions in *Learn the language* on the previous Student Book page.

- Put students into pairs and explain the speaking activity.

- Encourage students to add details about the stories they tell.

Model conversation

A Her cousin invited her to spend Christmas with her.
B What did she do?
A She spent the whole day partying at the beach.
B Sounds great.

Extension

Have pairs describe another festival or holiday they have celebrated to each other.

Unit 2

Listening task two

A **1** **25** Listen for main ideas The speaker is talking about harvest festivals around the world. Listen and choose the statements that best summarize the main points in the talk.

A Nowadays, most people do not depend on a good harvest for survival, but continue to celebrate the gathering of the harvest.

B Nowadays, people depend on a good harvest for survival, but not many countries celebrate the gathering of the harvest.

C Most harvest festivals include a big feast for all members of the family.

D The purpose of the harvest festivals is to give thanks for the good harvest.

E The purpose of the harvest festivals is to eat special food and watch the full moon.

B **1** **25** Listen for comparison and contrast What do the festivals have in common? What are the differences? Listen again and check ☑ the correct information in the table below.

	Chuseok	Onam	Mid-Autumn Festival	Yam Festival
honor ancestors	✓			✓
give thanks to the gods				✓
watch the full moon			✓	
eat special food	✓	✓	✓	✓
watch boat races		✓		
sing and dance	✓			✓
play drums				✓
women wear their best "hanbok"	✓			

Speak out! **1** **25** Work with a partner. Choose two of the festivals. Listen again and take notes about them. Think about the similarities and differences between them. Talk about them with your partner.

Both festivals take place during the harvest season. Both festivals celebrate the gathering of the harvest. But in Korea, the special food is ... while in Ghana, people eat dishes made from ...

16

Listening task two

- The new language introduced in this section includes the following words and phrases:

      depended on
      survival
      during the harvest season
      graves
      boat races
      row large boats
      ancient
      watching the full moon
      'mooncakes'
      ceremonies
      give thanks to the gods
      drums

- Ask students what they know of any popular harvest festivals. What do people do at these festivals?

- Explain that students will listen to a talk about harvest festivals around the world. Have students read through the statements first.

- Play the audio (CD1, track 25) and have students choose the statements that summarize the main points.

- Ask students to say what they can remember about one or more of the festivals. They can use the pictures at the bottom of the page as prompts.

Audio script [CD1, track 25]

Lecturer People from different cultures all over the world celebrate the gathering of the harvest. Many harvest festivals began a long time ago—probably as early as people began farming. Planting and harvest times were very important to early farmers because they depended on a good harvest for survival. Nowadays, people around the world still continue to celebrate a good harvest. These are some of the harvest festivals celebrated in different parts of the world.

Chuseok is a Korean festival that takes places during the harvest season. Families travel to the graves of their ancestors and offer them rice and fruit. There is a special feast which starts with a family gathering where special rice cakes are served. Women, wearing their best 'hanbok', make a circle and sing and dance.

In India, people celebrate the Hindu festival of Onam in August or September. Many special activities begin before the actual holiday and last for ten days. One of the main traditions of Onam is the boat races. Men row large boats covered with red umbrellas. There is a big feast where around thirteen vegetarian dishes are served on banana leaves.

The Mid-Autumn Festival is celebrated in September or October when the ancient Chinese believed the moon was at its brightest and fullest. The festival is a time for families to gather for picnics or special dinners while watching the full moon. People eat different kinds of round cakes called 'mooncakes'.

In many parts of Africa, people celebrate during the harvest times. In Ghana, there is a fruits festival called the Yam Festival. The celebrations begin with ceremonies to honor the ancestors and give thanks to the gods for a good harvest. Special dishes made from yams are served at a big feast. People sing and dance to the sound of drums.

B

- Have students go over the information in the table.

- Play the audio (CD1, track 25) again and have students check the correct information.

- Put students into pairs and have them compare their answers.

- Review the answers with students by playing the audio again.

Speak out!

- The aim of this section is to integrate listening with other skills. In this case, students practice note-taking before doing verbal comparisons.

- Put students into pairs and explain the speaking activity.

- Play the audio (CD1, track 25) once more and have students take notes.

- Have students work in pairs to talk about the festivals with each other. Encourage students to add any extra details they might know about each festival, particularly if it is from their country.

2

Write what you hear

A **1** **26** The sounds /s/ and /z/ at the end of words may be difficult to hear because they often link to the sound that follows. Listen and complete the sentences.

Example: We had lots‿of ice‿cream. → We had ____*lots of ice cream*____.

1 I want to try something different ____*this year*____.

2 Sydney ____*was amazing*____!

3 I woke up to ____*birds singing*____ outside my window.

4 Special ____*rice cakes are*____ served.

5 Special ____*dishes made*____ from ____*yams are*____ served at a big feast.

6 Chuseok is a Korean festival that ____*takes place*____ during the harvest season.

7 I ____*always spend Christmas*____ with my family.

8 The ____*celebrations begin*____ with ____*ceremonies*____ to honor the ancestors.

B **1** **26** Now listen again and repeat. Try saying the sentences as naturally as possible.

Use what you learn

A Try to remember one of your own festival or holiday stories. Write notes, using the questions below to help you.

- What holiday/festival was special for you?
- Where were you?
- What happened?
- When did it happen?
- What did you do?
- How did you feel?

Answers may vary.

– New Year's Eve in Osaka

– special → wore my kimono, went to shrine at midnight, rang the bell

– New Year's Day → ate special food w/ family

B Work in small groups. Talk about festivals or holidays that were special for you.

A What holiday was special for you?
B New Year.
C Where were you?
B I was in Japan.
D What happened?
B We ate different kinds of special food.

17

Write what you hear

Aim

The aim of this section is for students to distinguish between and correctly pronounce the sounds /s/ and /z/ at the end of words when they link to the sound that follows.

The letters "s", "ss" and "c" are often pronounced as /s/, while the letter "z" is usually pronounced as /z/. However, in words like *was* and *is*, "s" is pronounced as /z/. In words like *faces* and *races*, when "c" appears between vowels sounds, it is pronounced as /s/.

The sounds /s/ and /z/ differ only in terms of voice: /s/ is a voiceless sound while /z/ is a voiced sound. It is easy to tell the difference as voiced sounds usually have a buzzing sound in the throat while voiceless sounds do not. However, /s/ and /z/ may be difficult to distinguish at the end of a word because the buzzing sound of /z/ is often not as strong as other positions, like the beginning or middle of a word. The sounds /s/ and /z/ often link to a following vowel sound. For example, *We had lots of* (/lɑːtsəv/) *ice cream. Chuseok is a* (/ɪzə/) *Korean festival.*

- Introduce the sounds /s/ and /z/ at the end of words. Explain the difference between the two sounds.

- Point out the example and model the sentence.

- Play the audio (CD1, track 26) and have students fill in the missing words.

- Review the answers by playing the audio again. Encourage students to find and correct any of their mistakes.

Audio script [CD1, track 26]

Example: We had lots of ice cream.
1 I want to try something different this year.
2 Sydney was amazing!
3 I woke up to birds singing outside my window.
4 Special rice cakes are served.
5 Special dishes made from yams are served at a big feast.
6 Chuseok is a Korean festival that takes place during the harvest season.
7 I always spend Christmas with my family.
8 The celebrations begin with ceremonies to honor the ancestors.

- Play the audio (CD1, track 26) again. Have students repeat the sentences out loud, paying special attention to the pronunciation of the sounds /s/ and /z/ at the end of the words.

- Monitor and provide feedback on students' pronunciation.

Extension

Have pairs of students find as many different words as they can with different spellings for the sounds /s/ and /z/. Have some pairs read their words to the class.

Use what you learn

Aim

The aim of this section is to give students the opportunity to talk about a holiday or festival story of their own.

- Review the unit vocabulary and functional language by asking students to tell you what they know about a local festival or holiday.

- Have students work individually to think of what they would say to answer the six questions about their festival or holiday story.

- Explain the activity and model the sentences at the bottom of the page with three students.

- Put students into small groups and have them work together to complete the activity. Encourage group members to ask follow-up questions to keep each person's story from finishing too quickly.

Your score:

_____ /9

Test yourself

1 **27** **You will hear three short talks. You will be asked to answer three questions about each talk. Choose the best response to each question.**

1 What do many holidays have in common?

- **A** Leaves and branches.
- **B** Christmas wreaths.
- **C** Decorations.
- **D** They are held at the same time of year.

2 At what special events were wreaths used in the past?

- **A** Christmas and the Water Festival.
- **B** The Olympic Games and Roman festivals.
- **C** English and Greek festivals.
- **D** When people died.

3 Who wore wreaths on their heads in Roman times?

- **A** Women and children.
- **B** Men and children.
- **C** Children.
- **D** Women.

4 What is the most common way of celebrating a festival?

- **A** Having a long holiday.
- **B** Eating together at a feast.
- **C** Having several main courses.
- **D** Eating traditional harvest foods.

5 What do people usually eat at Thanksgiving in the United States?

- **A** Turkey for the main course and Christmas pie for dessert.
- **B** Harvest foods for the main course and dessert.
- **C** Turkey for the main course and pumpkin pie for dessert.
- **D** Turkey pie for the main course and yams for dessert.

6 Which of the following foods is NOT mentioned by the speaker?

- **A** Potatoes and carrots.
- **B** Pumpkin and yams.
- **C** Seafood and salad.
- **D** Turkey and rice.

7 What kinds of people enjoy the Slow Food Festival?

- **A** People who like fast food.
- **B** People who don't mind taking their time to make their favorite foods.
- **C** People who don't like to eat quickly.
- **D** People who don't like to eat slowly.

8 How many farmers, fishermen and other people come to the festival?

- **A** 128.
- **B** About 2,000.
- **C** Less than 5,000.
- **D** More than 5,000.

9 Why were there lots of pasta dishes at the festival?

- **A** Pasta dishes are very popular.
- **B** The festival was held in Italy.
- **C** There were many Italian chefs.
- **D** Pasta dishes are easy to make.

18

Test yourself

Aim

The aim of this section is to provide exam practice. Students will listen to three short talks, each followed by three questions, and choose the correct answer from four answer choices.

Explain the test format. Students will have seven seconds after each question to choose the correct answer. They should read the questions and the answer choices first to have an idea of what details they should listen for.

Audio script [CD1, track 27]

Questions 1 through 3 refer to the following talk.

Woman   Most holidays have one thing in common: special decorations. People use decorations to change the look of their homes. It's a way of telling other people that you are celebrating the holiday. In some countries, the most common decorations are natural things, such as the leaves or branches from trees. At Christmas, branches, leaves and other things are formed into a circle, called a wreath. A wreath hanging on the door at Christmas reminds people that spring will come again. Wreaths are also used at other times as well, such as to remember people who have died. In fact, the wreath is a very old tradition, older than Christmas. Greek athletes in the first Olympic Games wore wreaths when they won a race. In Roman times, women wore wreaths on their heads during festivals. Nowadays, in some cultures, women still wear wreaths on their heads during weddings.

1   What do many holidays have in common?
2   At what special events were wreaths used in the past?
3   Who wore wreaths on their heads in Roman times?

Questions 4 through 6 refer to the following talk.

Man   One of the most popular ways of celebrating a holiday or festival is to have a feast. People enjoy eating together, and big meals are common all around the world. At many harvest festivals people eat traditional harvest foods that are gathered during the fall. Harvest foods served during fall or winter feasts include pumpkin, potatoes and carrots. These feasts often feature special foods that are only served once or twice a year. At Thanksgiving in the United States it's traditional to eat turkey as a main course and pumpkin pie for dessert. Other cultures have their own foods. For example, people throughout Asia usually have feasts that serve rice dishes. In some African countries, foods made from yams are served at the harvest feasts.

4   What is the most common way of celebrating a festival?
5   What do people usually eat at Thanksgiving in the United States?
6   Which of the following foods is NOT mentioned by the speaker?

Questions 7 through 9 refer to the following talk.

Woman   This year I went to the Turin Slow Food Festival. Everyone knows about fast food: inexpensive foods prepared very quickly. Slow food is just the opposite and the Slow Food Festival is for people who don't mind taking their time to make their favorite foods and like to use fresh meat and vegetables. The festival is popular with more than five thousand people from a hundred and twenty-eight countries such as farmers, fishermen and others who gather or make food. They come together to celebrate traditional foods and enjoy eating their favorite dishes as well as new ones. Because the festival was in Italy, there were lots of Italians there and lots of pasta dishes. There were also different kinds of pizza and other Italian foods. The only difficult thing was talking to people … Greek, Russian, Arabic, Chinese, Japanese, Korean … so many different languages.

7   What kinds of people enjoy the Slow Food Festival?
8   How many farmers, fishermen and other people come to the festival?
9   Why were there lots of pasta dishes at the festival?

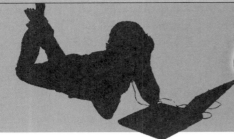

Go online!

Visit the *Sounds Good* website at **www.sounds-good-online.com**
Click on **Go online!** for extra listening practice.

Online listening

A *1* **28** `Listen for feelings` Jennifer is talking to her friend Marc about Christmas. Listen and check the things Jennifer says she likes.

B *1* **28** `Listen for cause and effect` Listen again and choose the best answers.

1 Jennifer doesn't like getting a tree because …

   A she does not like the smell.
   B it's too expensive.
   (C) she does not like the cold weather.

2 Jennifer cried one year after putting the decorations on the tree one year because …

   A the tree caught on fire.
   B Jennifer's cat knocked it over.
   (C) Jennifer's dog knocked it over.

3 Jennifer doesn't like parades because …

   A there are too many people.
   (B) she doesn't like the weather.
   C they are boring.

4 Jennifer didn't like Santa when she was young because …

   A he didn't bring her any gifts.
   (B) she was scared of him.
   C she didn't like to go to the mall.

Download *Sounds Good* Podcast 26

Now listen to Podcast 26. You can do the activities, read the transcript, or simpy enjoy listening to young people from around the world.

19

Go online!

Students can visit the *Sounds Good* website at *www.sounds-good-online.com* and click on *Go online!* for extra listening practice based on the unit topic.

Online listening

This section can be used in two ways.

Students can use this for some optional, self-study listening practice outside the classroom. Students will see the same activity as printed in their Student Book and they will be able to complete it online, with immediate feedback on their answer choices.

Alternatively, you can use this section in class as an extension activity. The Online listening is recorded on the Class CDs for this purpose.

Students will listen to a conversation between Maro and Jennifer. Jennifer is talking about how she feels about Christmas. Marc has a Canadian accent.

Audio script [CD1, track 28]

Marc	Merry Christmas, Jennifer.
Jennifer	Merry Christmas? I hate Christmas.
Marc	What? How can you hate Christmas? How can anyone hate Christmas?
Jennifer	I hate everything about it.
Marc	I don't believe you. I love Christmas. I remember when I was a little kid, my parents and I used to go and get a Christmas tree. The smell was wonderful.
Jennifer	Oh, yeah, I love a tree, but not going out to buy one when it's freezing outside.
Marc	You don't like winter?
Jennifer	I hate winter. It's cold and snowy. Or worse, it's cold and rainy. And what does everyone do before Christmas? They spend all their time and money at the shopping mall buying gifts. I don't really like shopping.
Marc	I don't like shopping either, but I like the snow and the cold weather. It's a great time of year for skiing.
Jennifer	Oh, I don't like to ski.
Marc	OK, so maybe you don't like skiing or the cold weather, but you can always ask someone to get your Christmas tree. Then you can put on all the lovely decorations. That's always fun.
Jennifer	Yeah, I remember. One year we spent an hour or two putting all the decorations on the tree. I love decorations, but …
Marc	But?
Jennifer	But that year my dog knocked the tree over and half of them broke. I cried.
Marc	Oh, bad luck. But what about the Christmas parade?
Jennifer	I told you, I don't like the weather so I don't like parades either.
Marc	But you can watch it on TV.
Jennifer	To tell you the truth, when I was little, I was scared of Santa. A big man in a red suit? I cried every year.
Marc	Well, there must be something you like about Christmas.
Jennifer	Yeah … I like getting gifts!

Podcast 26

Encourage students to download Podcast 26. Inspired by the unit topic, it is authentic and high-interest, and features young people from around the world.

3

I can't stand the graffiti.

Goals
- Identifying the pros and cons of city and country life
- Understanding environmental issues

Learn the language

A 🔘 1 29 **Which of the following things are bad for the environment? Match the words to the pictures. Then listen and check your answers.**

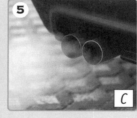

A	advertisements
B	litter
C	car fumes
D	organic vegetables
E	noise pollution
F	recycled products
G	garbage
H	air pollution
I	factory smoke
J	graffiti

FOCUS

B 🔘 1 30 **Listen and choose the answer you hear.**

1 Have you always lived in the city?

- **A** Yes, I have.
- **(B)** No, I grew up in a small town.

2 What's the best part of living in the city?

- **(A)** I suppose it's the arts festivals.
- **B** There are lots of places like museums to visit.

3 Anything you don't like about the city?

- **(A)** I can't stand the litter and graffiti.
- **B** Who wants to smell car fumes all the time?

4 Why did you decide to get out of the city?

- **A** I got tired of seeing advertisements everywhere.
- **(B)** The noise drove me crazy.

20

Unit overview

The topic of this unit is city and country life as well as environmental issues. In Listening task one, students will listen to David interviewing two people about what they like and dislike about living in the city and the country. In Listening task two, students will listen to a lecture about the green city of the future. In the speaking activities, students will have an opportunity to talk about what they like and dislike about the place where they live.

Learn the language

- Ask students what they like and dislike about city life and/or country life. Where would they prefer to live? Why? Make some notes on the board.

- Have students open the book and look at the pictures. Ask them what is shown in each picture.

- Read the words (A–J) and ask students to match them to the pictures.

- Review the words for environmental issues to make sure that students understand them all.

- Allow students a few minutes to finish writing the answers.

- Play the audio (CD1, track 29) and have students check their answers. Stop the CD and play each sentence again as often as necessary.

Audio script [CD1, track 29]

1   Air pollution. There was a lot of air pollution.
2   Garbage. There was garbage floating in the river.
3   Litter. There was litter on the streets.
4   Factory smoke. There was a lot of factory smoke.
5   Car fumes. You could smell car fumes.
6   Advertisements. There were advertisements everywhere.
7   Graffiti. There was graffiti on the buildings.
8   Noise pollution. There was a lot of noise pollution.
9   Organic vegetables. I grow organic vegetables in a small garden.
10 Recycled products. I try to buy recycled products.

B

- Ask students the questions in the *Focus* box to elicit some possible answers.

- Have students read through the sentences and the answer choices to get an idea of what they will be listening for. Explain that none of the answers are wrong, but only one answer is spoken on the audio so students cannot simply guess the answers.

- Play the audio (CD1, track 30) and have students choose the answer they hear.

- Review the answers by playing the audio again.

- Have students role-play the questions and answers in the *Focus* box.

Language note

Fumes are a gas or smoke with a strong smell which is unpleasant to breathe in. *Smoke* is a white, grey or black gas that is produced by burning something.

Audio script [CD1, track 30]

1
Man   Have you always lived in the city?
Woman No, I grew up in a small town.

2
Woman What's the best part of living in the city?
Man   I suppose it's the arts festivals.

3
Man   Anything you don't like about the city?
Woman I can't stand the litter and graffiti.

4
Woman Why did you decide to get out of the city?
Man   The noise drove me crazy.

3

Listening task one

A **1** 31-32 [Listen for gist] David is interviewing two people for a survey. One person lives in the city and the other lives in the country. Read the four summaries. Listen and check ☑ the summary that best matches each conversation.

1

☐ I don't like living in the city because of all the advertisements and graffiti, but I like the music festivals.

☑ I like living in the city. It's exciting and there are lots of different things to do. But I really don't like the litter and pollution.

2

☐ I have always lived in the country and I love it here. I walk past a river to work. I think the country is a healthy place to live.

☑ I didn't grow up in the country but I love living here now. I mostly work at home. I think the city is an unhealthy place to live.

B **1** 31-32 [Listen for feelings] Listen again and write [+] for the things they like and [−] for the things they don't like. There are two extra things for each person.

1

_+_ places to visit

____ shopping malls

_+_ music festivals

_−_ graffiti

_−_ air pollution

_−_ noise pollution

____ smell in the city

2

_−_ advertisements

_−_ river in the city

_−_ smell in the city

____ noise in the city

_−_ air pollution

____ graffiti

_+_ smell of farm animals

Speak out!

Work with a partner. Choose one of the speakers above and have your partner ask you questions about the things they like or don't like about the city and/or the country.

Use the language in **FOCUS** to help you.

21

Listening task one

- Introduce the character, David, who is conducting a survey of people's attitudes towards living in the city and the country. The man in the first interview on track 31 has a British accent.

- Have students read through the summaries on the page quickly.

- Play the audio (CD1, tracks 31–32) and have students check the best summary for each conversation.

- Review the answers with students.

- Ask students whether they think the people being interviewed are typical of people who live in the city or the country.

Audio script [CD1, tracks 31–32]

1

David	Could I ask you a few questions?
Man	OK.
David	Thanks. So, have you always lived in the city?
Man	No, I grew up in a small town in England. I came here to go to university and then got a job.
David	What's the best part of living in the city?
Man	The best part? Mm … it's hard to say just one thing. The city's exciting. There's always something going on. You can do whatever you want, whenever you want. There are lots of places to visit. But you're asking for just one thing. I suppose it's the different events. I like music a lot and there are a few music festivals every year.
David	Anything you don't like?
Man	Um, let's see. I really can't stand the litter and graffiti. Pollution is a real problem too, and not just air pollution. The noise pollution is bad. Sometimes it's so noisy you can't sleep.

2

David	Nice little village! You like it here?
Woman	Love it.
David	Could I ask you a few questions?
Woman	OK.
David	Have you always lived in the country?
Woman	No, I moved here just a few years ago. I used to live in the city but then I got a new job with a computer company. Now I mostly work from home so I can live anywhere. I decided to get out of the city before it drove me crazy.
David	What didn't you like?

Woman	Oh, lots of little things. I got tired of seeing advertisements everywhere. I walked to work past a river with garbage floating in it. It's kind of sad. And, of course, the air pollution. It's not just that it smells, it's unhealthy. Who wants to walk around smelling car fumes and factory smoke all the time?
David	Uh … speaking of smells …
Woman	Oh, that's just the farm animals. That smell doesn't bother me.

- Play the audio (CD1, tracks 31–32) again. Ask students to identify whether each speaker feels positively or negatively about the different aspects of city and country life by writing "+" for the things they like and "–" for the things they don't like.

- Review the answers with students. If necessary, play the audio again.

Speak out!

- Review the language in the *Focus* box on the previous Student Book page.

- Put students into pairs and explain the speaking activity.

- Encourage students to talk about other aspects of life in the country or the city that they feel positively or negatively about.

Model conversation

A Has this man always lived in the city?
B No. He grew up in a small town in England.
A What's the best part of living in the city?
B He says it's the different events.
A Anything he doesn't like?
B He can't stand the litter and graffiti.

Extension

Have pairs pretend that one person is from the country and the other is from the city. Each partner is trying to convince the other partner that he or she should move.

Unit 3

Listening task two

Ⓐ **1** `33` Listen for main ideas The speaker is talking about the green city of the future. Listen and number the pictures in the order each thing is mentioned. There is one extra picture.

recycling

building local parks

creating less pollution when traveling

organic food

using environmentally friendly energy

Ⓑ **1** `33` Listen for opinions Listen again and check ☑ the opinions that you hear.

1 Being green means the same thing to everybody. ☐

2 Local food is healthier for you. ☑

3 Organic food tastes better. ☑

4 Environmentally friendly energy is expensive. ☐

5 Recycling saves money. ☑

6 By building green cities, people will preserve the environment. ☑

Speak out!

1 `33` Work with a partner. Look at the list of environmental problems below. Does the speaker offer any solutions to these problems? Listen again and write some solutions to the problems listed below. Discuss your answers with your partner.

1 Air pollution from factory smoke *use environmentally friendly energy*

2 Too much garbage *buy recycled products*

3 Air pollution from car fumes *smaller cities; more access to public transportation; pedestrian areas and bike lanes*

22

Listening task two

- The new language introduced in this section includes the following words and phrases:

      buying organic food
      using environmentally friendly energy
      recycling
      creating less pollution
      community gardens
      resources
      affect the environment
      electricity
      processing materials
      manufacturing new products
      reduce waste
      preserve our environment

- Ask students what sorts of things would impove the environment of a city. Have they done any of these practices? Brainstorm some ideas on the board.

- Have students look at the pictures and say what is shown in each picture.

- Explain that students will listen to a lecture about the green city of the future. Explain what green means in this context. The lecture will mention all except one of the things in the pictures.

- Play the audio (CD1, track 33) and have students number the pictures.

- Ask students what needs to be done in the green city of the future, e.g., *All vegetables will be organic; People will use environmentally friendly energy.*

Language note

In this context, *green* is used to signify something that is environmental or ecological.

Audio script [CD1, track 33]

Lecturer

Today, I'm going to talk about the green city of the future. Being green means different things to different people. To some people, it means buying organic food or using environmentally friendly energy. To other people, it means recycling. When some people think about being green, they think of creating less pollution when they travel. These four meanings of green will shape the city of the future. Let me briefly explain each one.

First, all vegetables will be organic and grown in community gardens. Most people believe local food is healthier for you and better for the environment. I think organic food generally tastes better too.

Second, environmentally friendly energy uses resources such as the wind or the sun so it doesn't affect the environment. In the green city of the future, wind and sunshine will provide all the electricity that people need.

Third, people will buy recycled products. Recycling means collecting and processing materials that are used for manufacturing new products. Recycling will reduce waste and save money.

Finally, people will try to find ways to create less pollution when they travel. Green cities will be smaller so people can work close to home or at home. There will be more access to public transportation so people won't need cars. Pedestrian areas and bike lanes will make it easy to walk or cycle around the city.

For the green city to work, everyone has to help. From government to businesses and people at home, everyone has to make buying organic food, using environmentally friendly energy, recycling and creating less pollution part of their daily routine. In this way, I believe we will be able to preserve our environment.

- Have students read through the sentences quickly and think about whether they are mentioned in the lecture.

- Play the audio (CD1, track 33) again and have students check the opinions they hear.

- Review the answers with students.

Speak out!

- The aim of this section is to integrate listening with other skills. In this case, students practice note-taking before discussing solutions.

- Put students into pairs and explain the speaking activity.

- Have students look at the list of environmental problems and think about whether the lecturer offers any solutions to these problems.

- Play the audio (CD1, track 33) once more and have students write the solutions to the problems.

- Have pairs discuss their answers with each other. Encourage them to add solutions of their own.

Model conversation

A What's one solution to air pollution from factory smoke?
B Factories will need to use environmentally friendly energy.
A Yes. I have another solution: make the factories pay a green tax. Then that money can be used to develop environmentally friendly energy.

Write what you hear

A **1 34** The sounds /t/ and /d/ at the end of words may be difficult to hear. They may be silent, blend together with or link to the sound that follows. Listen and complete the sentences.

Example: (You like it here?) ➔ You like ___*it here*___ ?

(The best part?) ➔ The ___*best part*___ ?

1 ___*Could I*___ ask you a few questions?

2 What ___*didn't you*___ like?

3 I really ___*can't stand*___ the litter and graffiti.

4 I ___*moved here just a*___ few years ago.

5 I ___*used to*___ live in the city, but then I ___*got a*___ new job.

6 I ___*decided to get out*___ of the city before ___*it drove*___ me crazy.

7 It's ___*not just that it smells*___ , it's unhealthy.

8 People will try to ___*find ways to create less*___ pollution.

B **1 34** Now listen again and repeat. Try saying the sentences as naturally as possible.

Use what you learn

A Are you from the country or the city? What do you like about it? What drives you crazy? Write at least three things you like and three things you don't like.

(*Answers may vary.*)

I like …	I don't like …
that there's no air pollution.	the smell of farm animals.
that there's no noise pollution.	the long commute to school.
the space.	that it's a bit boring.

B Work in small groups. Talk about what you like or dislike about the place where you live. Take turns.

A Where do you live?
B I live in the country.
C What are the things you like about it?
B There's no air pollution.
D Anything that drives you crazy?
B I can't stand the smell of farm animals.

23

Write what you hear

Aim

The aim of this section is for students to recognize and correctly pronounce the sounds /t/ and /d/ at the end of words in sentences.

The letters 't' and 'd' are pronounced as the sounds /t/ and /d/: /t/ is a voiceless sound while /d/ is a voiced sound. The sounds /t/ and /d/ at the end of words are not always pronounced clearly. They are sometimes silent or blend together with the first sound in the following word. For example, the /d/ sound in *I used to* is silent, while in *I moved_here*, /d/ blends with /h/ to sound like /t/. When preceded or followed by a similar consonant sound, the sounds /t/ and /d/ are sometimes silent. For example, *last night, find ways*.

- Introduce the sounds /t/ and /d/ at the end of words and explain about their pronunciation.
- Point out the example and model the sentences. Explain that the 't' in the word *best* is sometimes silent.
- Play the audio (CD1, track 34) and have students fill in the missing words.
- Review the answers by playing the audio again. Encourage students to find and correct any of their mistakes.

Audio script [CD1, track 34]

Example: You like it here?   The best part?
1   Could I ask you a few questions?
2   What didn't you like?
3   I really can't stand the litter and graffiti.
4   I moved here just a few years ago.
5   I used to live in the city, but then I got a new job.
6   I decided to get out of the city before it drove me crazy.
7   It's not just that it smells, it's unhealthy.
8   People will try to find ways to create less pollution.

B

- Play the audio (CD1, track 34) again. This time, ask students to repeat each sentence out loud paying special attention to the pronunciation of the sounds /t/ and /d/ at the end of words in the sentences. Meanwhile, remind students to try to say the sentences as naturally as possible.
- Monitor and provide feedback on students' pronunciation.

Use what you learn

Aim

The aim of this section is to give students the opportunity to talk about what they like and dislike about the place they live.

- Review the unit vocabulary and functional language by asking students what the best and worst things are about the city and the country.
- Have students work individually to fill in the table.

- Explain the activity and model the sentences at the bottom of the page with three students.
- Put students into small groups and have them work together to complete the activity. Encourage groups to talk about the reason for their likes and dislikes.

Extension

Ask students to survey each other and make a list of the reasons why city life or country life is better. Then have them report back to the class.

Model conversation
A   The main reason people want to live in the country is the clean environment.
B   But living in the country is not as exciting as living in the city. There are lots of places to go in the city.

Unit **3**

Test yourself

1 **35** You will hear a discussion in an environmental studies class. You may take notes while you listen. You will be asked to answer six questions of different kinds. You may use your notes to answer the questions.

1 What is the main topic of the discussion?

A How to create more environmentally friendly areas.
B How to start recycling programs.
C How to reduce air pollution.
(D) How to save energy and resources.

2 Do the students discuss the following things? For each statement, check ☑ the YES or NO column.

	YES	NO
People can save energy by using cars that create less pollution.		✓
People can save energy by using smaller cars.	✓	
People can save energy by using public transportation.	✓	
People can save energy by turning off electrical appliances when they are not using them.	✓	
People can save energy by using resources such as water or wood.		✓

3 Which of the following ideas are found in the discussion? Choose two responses.

(A) Turning off lights at home can save energy.
B People shouldn't waste paper.
(C) There should be more recycling programs.
D Sharing car rides to work can save energy.

4 What green idea do they NOT talk about?

A Making pedestrian-friendly areas.
B Leaving cars at home.
(C) Growing organic food.
D Developing wind power.

5 What way of saving resources do the students NOT mention?

A Recycling the materials that we use.
B Starting recycling programs.
(C) Re-using plastic bags.
D Buying products with less packaging.

6 How does the professor feel about the students' responses?

A Their responses are not correct.
B She hopes the students can do better next time.
(C) Their responses are very good.
D Their responses are not very good.

Test yourself

Aim

The aim of this section is to provide exam practice. Students will listen to a discussion and then answer six questions of different kinds.

Explain the test format. Students will have seven seconds after each question to answer the question. Students should read the questions and answers first so they have a general idea of the types of information they will listen for. While listening to the discussion, students may take notes of key points to help them answer the questions. Explain that the first question is a gist question. The gist may be directly stated in the listening extract or students may be required to bring together information from different sections of the extract in order to understand the main topic of the discussion.

Point out that apart from traditional multiple-choice questions with four answer choices and a single correct answer, there are other question types such as questions that require students to match text to two categories in a table and questions with two answers.

The last question asks students about the professor's attitude which is not directly stated. In order to answer this question, they should not only listen to what it is said but how it is said and draw a conclusion about the speaker's attitude.

Point out that the first male student speaking in the discussion has a British accent.

Audio script [CD1, track 35]

Lecturer We face a lot of environmental challenges—dirty air and water, litter on the streets and garbage floating in rivers, lots of traffic and not much open space. People complain about air, water and noise pollution, and talk about greener living. Greener living means saving resources. Let's start with energy. How can we save energy? Any ideas?

Woman I think we can start by saving energy on the road. We should use smaller cars and keep them in good condition.

Man 1 Why don't we just leave our cars at home? We can use public transportation or cycle or walk …

Woman Cycling is not always possible. It's even dangerous sometimes where there are no bike lanes or the pedestrian lanes are too narrow.

Lecturer That's a good point. I think we need to make our area more pedestrian- and bike-friendly so people will walk and ride their bikes. How about saving energy at home?

Man 2 We can start by turning off the lights and other electrical appliances when we aren't using them.

Man 3 Yes, but that's not enough. I believe that we should develop environmentally friendly energy sources such as the sun or the wind.

Lecturer These are excellent ideas about saving energy. Now let's think about ways of saving our resources.

Man 1 The most important thing is to start recycling the materials that we use. Recycling saves resources, cuts energy use, and reduces water and air pollution.

Man 3 Yes, but not all cities have recycling programs, and not all people make an effort to sort their trash and take items such as paper or glass to a recycling center.

Lecturer That's why we need to encourage local governments and businesses to start recycling programs.

Woman But not all people buy recycled products because they are more expensive.

Man 2 Yes, you're right. Perhaps we can encourage people to buy products with less packaging. Most packaging is wasteful and unnecessary.

Lecturer OK. I think we've got some very good ideas about greener living and how to save energy and resources. I want you to write them down for our next study session and perhaps add a few more. Thanks, and see you the day after tomorrow.

1   What is the main topic of the discussion?
2   Do the students discuss the following things?
3   Which of the following ideas are found in the discussion?
4   What green idea do they NOT talk about?
5   What way of saving resources do the students NOT mention?
6   How does the professor feel about the students' responses?

3 I can't stand the graffiti.

Go online!

Visit the *Sounds Good* website at **www.sounds-good-online.com**
Click on **Go online!** for extra listening practice.

Online listening

A **1** **36** Listen for sequence Peter and Sheila are talking about the city. Listen and number the pictures in the order each thing is mentioned. There is one extra picture.

B **1** **36** Listen for specific information Listen again and complete the sentences.

1 Peter has lived in the city _____*all his life*_____ .

2 He _____*grew up*_____ here.

3 He does not like the city because there are many _____*problems*_____ now.

4 The streets are _____*full of garbage*_____ all the time.

5 There is a lot of pollution from _____*car fumes*_____ and factories.

6 Shopping and eating out are very _____*expensive*_____ now.

7 Peter _____*can't stand*_____ the country either.

Download *Sounds Good* Podcast 27

Now listen to Podcast 27. You can do the activities, read the transcript, or simply enjoy listening to young people from around the world.

25

Go online!

Students can visit the *Sounds Good* website at *www.sounds-good-online.com* and click on *Go online!* for extra listening practice based on the unit topic.

Online listening

This section can be used in two ways.

Students can use this for some optional, self-study listening practice outside the classroom. Students will see the same activity as printed in their Student Book and they will be able to complete it online, with immediate feedback on their answer choices.

Alternatively, you can use this section in class as an extension activity. The Online listening is recorded on the Class CDs for this purpose.

Students will listen to a conversation between Sheila and Peter, who are talking about the good and bad things about living in the city.

Audio script [CD1, track 36]

Sheila	So how long have you lived here, Peter?
Peter	In the city? All my life. I grew up here.
Sheila	Oh, you're so lucky. It's a great city.
Peter	Maybe for some people.
Sheila	Oh, come on. What's the best part of living in the city?
Peter	The best part? Huh, I … I don't know. It used to be a nice place to live, but there are so many problems now. I mean, who wants to walk around with the streets full of garbage all the time?
Sheila	There's not that much garbage, is there? I mean, I went to Central Park and—
Peter	Yeah, you probably didn't notice the garbage because there's so much pollution from car fumes and factories.
Sheila	Well, no more than most cities. I live out of town and it's true, the air's cleaner, but there's not so much to do. I mean, you've got all these great events in the city—
Peter	Oh, yeah. But it's pretty difficult to get tickets to go see anything. As soon as you see an advertisement, all the tickets are gone.
Sheila	But shopping? Restaurants?
Peter	Expensive. Everything's so expensive now.
Sheila	Is there anything you like?
Peter	Well, let me think … I don't think so. No, nothing special, really.

Sheila	So, if you don't like the city, why don't you move somewhere else … say, to a small town in the country?
Peter	Are you joking? I can't stand the country either.

Podcast 27

Encourage students to download Podcast 27. Inspired by the unit topic, it is authentic and high-interest, and features young people from around the world.

4 All the hard chores!

Goals
• Identifying chores
• Understanding duties

Learn the language

A **2 2** What chores do you have to do at home? Look at the pictures and complete the phrases with the words from the box. Then listen and check your answers.

> mop   feed   hang up   water   make   wash   vacuum   walk

1	**2**	**3**	**4**
walk the dog	*feed* the cat	*mop* the floor	*hang up* your clothes

5	**6**	**7**	**8**
make your bed	*water* the plants	*vacuum* your bedroom	*wash* the dishes

FOCUS

B **2 3** Listen and fill in the blanks with the phrases from the box.

> you could   remember to   don't forget   you'd better   it's time   you should

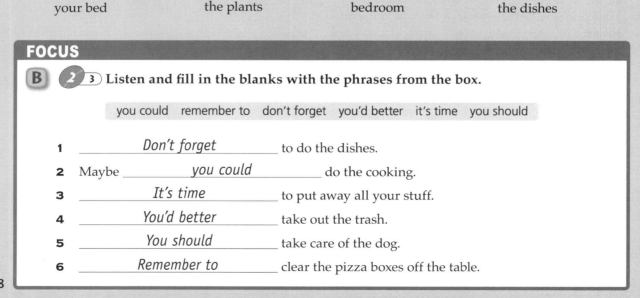

1. _____*Don't forget*_____ to do the dishes.
2. Maybe _____*you could*_____ do the cooking.
3. _____*It's time*_____ to put away all your stuff.
4. _____*You'd better*_____ take out the trash.
5. _____*You should*_____ take care of the dog.
6. _____*Remember to*_____ clear the pizza boxes off the table.

28

48

Unit overview

The topic of this unit is chores and duties around the house. In Listening task one, students will listen to Max and Jenny talking with their mother about chores to be done before discussing between themselves the chores each will do. In Listening task two, students will listen to Max and Jenny talking about the chores they need to do before their parents arrive home. In the speaking activities, students will have an opportunity to engage in both discussions and negotiations. They will also rank chores in order of importance and preference.

Learn the language

- Ask students what chores are important in their home and who in the family does each one. Ask them what sorts of chores they do regularly and which they share or do only occasionally.

- Have students open the book and look at the pictures. Ask them what chores are being illustrated in each picture.

- Read the words in the box and ask students to use them to complete the phrases under the pictures.

- Allow students a few minutes to finish writing the answers.

- Play the audio (CD2, track 2) and have students check their answers. Stop the CD and play each sentence again as often as necessary.

Language note

Explain the difference between *mop the floor* (with a wet mop) and *sweep* (with a dry broom). Instead of *hang up your clothes* we sometimes say *put away your clothes* but this can also refer to clothes that need to be folded and placed in drawers or on shelves.

Audio script [CD2, track 2]

1   Walk the dog. Don't forget to walk the dog.
2   Feed the cat. You need to feed the cat.
3   Mop the floor. You can mop the floor.
4   Hang up your clothes. Don't forget to hang up your clothes.
5   Make your bed. You need to make your bed.
6   Water the plants. Don't forget to water the plants.
7   Vacuum your bedroom. You can vacuum your bedroom.
8   Wash the dishes. You need to wash the dishes.

B

- Check students' comprehension of the words and phrases in the sentences: *do the dishes; do the cooking; put away; take out; take care; clear.*

- Discuss ways of asking people to do things. See which of the phrases students are unfamiliar with.

- Some of the answer phrases will work for different sentences, but only one response is spoken on the audio so students cannot simply guess the answers.

- Play the audio (CD2, track 3).

- Have students role-play the questions and answers in the *Focus* box.

Language note

You'd better is another way of saying *you should*. For example, *You'd better clean up your room.* In spoken English the 'd' is often deleted, so you hear *You better …*

Audio script [CD2, track 3]

1   Don't forget to do the dishes.
2   Maybe you could do the cooking.
3   It's time to put away all your stuff.
4   You'd better take out the trash.
5   You should take care of the dog.
6   Remember to clear the pizza boxes off the table.

4

Listening task one

A **2 4** Listen for gist Max and Jenny's mother is talking to them. What is she explaining? Listen and check ☑ the best summary.

1 The family is going away for two weeks and everyone needs to help. ☐

2 The parents are going away for two weeks and the kids need to take care of everything. ☑

3 The mother wants the kids to take care of the house when they have parties. ☐

B **2 5** Listen for specific information Jenny and Max have several chores to do. Which chores do they have to do? Listen and write J for Jenny or M for Max in each box.

M hang up your clothes
M make your bed
M put away all your stuff

M take care of the dog
J mop the kitchen floor
M take out the garbage

J water the plants
M vacuum the living room

C **2 5** Listen for key words Listen again and circle the correct words or phrases.

1 Let's (call up)/ phone all our friends and have a party!

2 Let's decide /(figure out) who does what.

3 Are you going to (do the cooking)/ cook the pizza ?

4 So no dishes to (wash)/ dry then.

5 And you need to do something about the kitchen / (your room).

6 You're leaving /(giving) me all the hard chores!

Speak out!

Work with a partner. Look at the above pictures and decide which chores you most and least like to do. Pretend you and your partner are in the same family and you are dividing the chores at home. Don't be afraid to say "No!"

Use the language in **FOCUS** to help you.

29

Listening task one

- Introduce the characters Jenny, Max and their mother. Explain that students will listen to a conversation between the three of them about different chores that need to be done.

- Play the audio (CD2, track 4).

- Ask students for their answers. What did they hear that helped them decide?

- Ask students how they think the mom feels.

Audio script [CD2, track 4]

Mom	Now, your dad and I will be gone for two weeks, so you're both in charge. Are you sure you can take care of everything and keep the house clean?
Jenny	Oh sure, Mom.
Max	Yeah, Mom. No problem.
Mom	OK. And don't forget to water the plants and walk the dog.
Max	Don't worry.
Mom	Now, don't leave all the dishes until the last minute—and no parties!
Jenny	Everything will be fine.

- Jenny and Max are dividing up the chores to be done. Ask students to discuss which are the most important ones.

- Play the audio (CD2, track 5).

- Ask students to write *M* for *Max* or *J* for *Jenny* next to the chores that each has to do. Review the answers with students.

Audio script [CD2, track 5]

Max	OK! They're gone! Let's call up all our friends and have a party!
Jenny	Max!
Max	Just kidding.
Jenny	Let's figure out who does what. Let's make a list of all the chores. We can each do half. You can take care of the dog. You have to walk him, and feed him.
Max	That's a lot. What are you going to do? Are you going to do the cooking?
Jenny	No, I don't have time for that. We can order pizza or something ...
Max	Good! So no dishes to wash then.

Jenny	But you better clean up. I'll mop the kitchen floor, but I don't want to do it every time you eat.
Max	Fine.
Jenny	Right. And you need to do something about your room.
Max	What's the matter with my room?
Jenny	Max! You need to hang up your clothes, make your bed and put away all your stuff ...
Max	OK. I can do that. Is that all?
Jenny	No, there's a lot more. Do you want to water the plants or vacuum the living room?
Max	I'll vacuum.
Jenny	Fine. I'll water the plants then. You take out the garbage.
Max	You're giving me all the hard chores!
Jenny	Yeah, but telling you what to do is one of my jobs.

Speak out!

- Review the language in the *Focus* box on the previous Student Book page.

- Put students into pairs and explain the speaking activity.

- Encourage students to talk about which chores they most and least like to do. Have pairs negotiate the chores that each will do.

Model conversation

A   Maybe you could vacuum the living room.
B   OK. I like vacuuming. What are you going to do?
A   I'll water the plants.
B   Don't forget to take out the trash.
A   I don't really like taking out the trash, but I'll do it. But you should mop the kitchen floor.

Unit 4

Listening task two

A **2** **6** Listen for sequence Jenny and Max have lots of cleaning to do before their parents get home. Number the problems in the order they mention them.

 4

sticky floor

 7

full trash can

 6

unmade bed

 5

broken glass

 1

floor not vacuumed

 3

pizza boxes not cleared

 2

dirty dishes

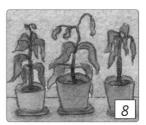 8

plants not watered

B **2** **6** Listen for key words Listen again and write the letter to match each sentence with the correct response.

1 They're coming home today? _C_

2 You vacuumed the floor, didn't you? _A_

3 You haven't even cleared the pizza boxes from the party two days ago. _F_

4 Sure, but your room is a complete mess. I can't even see the floor. _B_

5 Maybe you could take out the trash. _D_

6 What about watering the plants? _E_

A Uh, not really.

B It isn't so bad.

C That's right.

D That was your job!

E I watered them once or twice, I think.

F Big deal.

Speak out!

2 **6** Work with a partner. Listen again and make a list of Max and Jenny's problems. They don't have time to do all the chores. Number the chores in order of importance and discuss your answers with your partner.

30

Listening task two

- The new language introduced in this section includes the following phrases and sentences:

  > she expects the place to be spotless
  > spilled her drink all over the couch
  > kind of sticky
  > broken glass to clean up
  > your room is a complete mess
  > Let's just get everything done!
  > in the driveway

- Review the phrases and ask students to explain what is happening in each of the pictures, and what needs to be done.

- Explain that Max and Jenny's parents are arriving a day earlier and the house is in a mess. Students will listen to Jenny and Max's discussion about what needs to be done.

- Play the audio (CD2, track 6). Have students number the pictures in the order that they hear the chores.

- Ask students how they think Jenny and Max are feeling and what their mom will say when she sees the house.

Audio script [CD2, track 6]

Jenny	Max! Where have you been? Mom and Dad just called! They're coming home a day early!
Max	They're coming home today?
Jenny	That's right. And Mom says she expects the place to be spotless. You vacuumed the floor, didn't you?
Max	Uh, not really.
Jenny	Well, hurry. I need to do the dishes. You haven't even cleared the pizza boxes from the party two days ago.
Max	Big deal. Mom's really going to be mad that your friend spilled her drink all over the couch.
Jenny	I put a couple of pillows on top of it.
Max	Maybe you could try mopping the floor. It's kind of sticky. And I think there's some broken glass to clean up. I took care of the dog all by myself!
Jenny	Sure, but your room is a complete mess. I can't even see the floor!
Max	It isn't so bad. I put away my skateboard and some of my books. But, I'll hang up my clothes and make my bed. Maybe you could take out the trash.
Jenny	That was your job!

Max	It doesn't matter now. Let's just get everything done! What about watering the plants?
Jenny	I watered them once or twice, I think. But forget it, there's no time. Uh-oh ...
Max	Oh no! Is that their car in the driveway?

- Play the audio (CD2, track 6) again and have students match the sentences.

- Review the answers with students.

Speak out!

- The aim of this section is to integrate listening with other skills. In this case, students make a list and prioritize the chores before discussing with a partner.

- Put students into pairs and explain the speaking activity.

- Encourage students to talk about which chores are more important than others and decide which ones they should do first.

Model conversation

A The first thing to do is clean up the broken glass.

B I agree. It's dangerous. But then they should clear out the pizza boxes.

A No, they should mop the sticky floor next. Don't you agree?

B No, I don't.

Learn the rhythm

A ② ⑦ The pitch of our voice goes up or down at the end of statements and questions. This is called intonation. Listen and circle the correct intonation.

		Up	Down
Example:	Don't worry.	↗	(↘)
	Where have you been?	↗	(↘)
	Are you sure you can take care of everything?	(↗)	↘

1 Are you going to do the cooking? (↗) ↘   **5** They're coming home today? (↗) ↘

2 Everything will be fine. ↗ (↘)   **6** Is that their car in the driveway? (↗) ↘

3 What are you going to do? ↗ (↘)   **7** What's the matter with my room? ↗ (↘)

4 I'll water the plants then. ↗ (↘)   **8** They're coming home a day early! ↗ (↘)

B ② ⑦ Now listen again and repeat. Try saying the sentences with the correct intonation.

Use what you learn

A What are some of the chores at your home? Which ones do you not mind doing? Which ones do you not like doing? Answers may vary.

I don't mind …	I don't like …
– *washing the dishes* – *doing some of the cooking*	– *taking out the trash* – *cleaning the bathroom*

B Work in small groups. Talk about your list of chores and what you think of them. Have your group members ask you questions. Take turns.

A I don't mind washing the dishes, but I don't like taking out the trash.

B Why not?

A It smells.

C Who takes out the trash?

A My dad does.

31

Learn the rhythm

Aim

The aim of this section is for students to recognize and practice two intonation patterns: falling pitch on statements and *Wh*-questions and rising pitch on *Yes/No* questions.

Pitch refers to the high and low notes we make when we speak. We hear these high and low notes on certain stressed syllables. We use pitch changes at the end of a sentence to convey meaning or attitude. Pitch usually goes up at the end of a sentence when we ask a question that can be answered by *yes* or *no*. Pitch goes down at the end of a statement to show certainty or at the end of a question beginning with *Who, What, Where, When* and *How*.

- Introduce the topic: intonation and the change in pitch that occurs at the end of a sentence.

- Point out the example and model the three sentences and their pitch changes. Explain to students that they are to listen for the change in pitch at/near the end of the sentence.

- Play the audio (CD2, track 7) and have students circle the correct intonation.

- Play the audio again and review the answers. Encourage students to correct any of their mistakes.

Audio script [CD2, track 7]

Example: Don't worry.
Where have you been?
Are you sure you can take care of everything?

1   Are you going to do the cooking?
2   Everything will be fine.
3   What are you going to do?
4   I'll water the plants then.
5   They're coming home today?
6   Is that their car in the driveway?
7   What's the matter with my room?
8   They're coming home a day early!

- Play the audio (CD2, track 7) and have students repeat the sentences with the correct pitch.

- Monitor students' pronunciation and provide feedback on their pronunciation of falling and rising pitch.

Use what you learn

Aim

The aim of this section is to give students the opportunity to talk about chores they have to do at home and how they feel about them.

- Review the unit vocabulary and functional language by asking students for information about chores they do at home and elsewhere.

- Have students work individually to write a list of chores they don't mind, and chores they don't like.

B

- Explain the activity and model the sentences at the bottom of the page with three students.

- Put students into groups of three and have them work together to complete the activity.

- As with all pair and group speaking activities, move around the class, monitoring and facilitating where necessary.

- Follow up with the class on any points you heard and would like to highlight.

Unit 4

Your score:

_____ /9

Test yourself

2 **8** **You will hear three short conversations. You will be asked to answer three questions about each conversation. Choose the best response to each question.**

1 What sort of chores did the man have to do when he was young?

   A Hanging up his clothes and taking out the trash.
   B Washing the dishes and watering the plants.
   C Hanging up his clothes and watering the plants.
   D Washing the car and watering the plants.

2 What chore does the man especially hate doing?

   A Hanging up his clothes.
   B Washing the dishes.
   C Vacuuming.
   D Mopping the floor.

3 What is the man doing while mopping the floor and vacuuming?

   A Doing exercise.
   B Dancing.
   C Running.
   D Putting his books away.

4 What did the woman NOT mind doing when she was young?

   A Her mom's job.
   B Her dad's job.
   C Walking the dog.
   D Chores.

5 What did she start doing when she was older?

   A Watering other people's plants.
   B Vacuuming other people's floors.
   C Cleaning other people's houses.
   D Feeding other people's cats.

6 What will her staff do?

   A The chores you really don't like.
   B Feeding your cat and putting away your clothes.
   C The chores you really don't have time for.
   D Everything from feeding your cat to hanging up your clothes.

7 What are the first three things Rachel says she has to do?

   A Hang up her clothes, walk the dog and put away her CDs.
   B Take out the trash, hang up her clothes and put away her CDs.
   C Take out the trash, mop the floor and put away her CDs.
   D Vacuum the floor, hang up her clothes and put away her CDs.

8 What does Rachel want her friend to do?

   A Wash the dishes and take out the trash.
   B Mop the floor and wash the dishes.
   C Clean up the living room and hang up her clothes.
   D Mop the floor and put away the dishes.

9 What is Rachel going to do while her friend is in the kitchen?

   A Mop the kitchen floor.
   B Mop the bathroom floor.
   C Vacuum the living room.
   D Clean up her bedroom.

32

Test yourself

Aim

The aim of this section is to provide exam practice. Students will listen to three short conversations, each followed by three questions, and choose the correct answer from four answer choices.

Explain the test format. Students will have seven seconds after each question to choose the correct answer. Give them enough time to skim the questions and answer choices before listening.

Tell students that Rachel in the third conversation has a British accent.

Audio script [CD2, track 8]

Questions 1 through 3 refer to the following conversation.

Woman	I always hated doing chores.
Man	Me, too! When I was young, my mom always had a long list of chores for me ... washing the dishes, watering the plants ... that sort of thing.
Woman	But that was some time ago and now you live on your own. What do you do now?
Man	I still hate doing chores, especially vacuuming, but I've found a good way to get them done.
Woman	What's that?
Man	First, I set a time to do the chores. It's usually half an hour or an hour. Then I put on really loud music and I do the chores as quickly as I can. I turn mopping the floor and vacuuming my bedroom into dancing. I turn taking out the trash and putting away all my books into exercise. I don't take the dog for walks; I run. Doing chores is real fun now.

1 What sort of chores did the man have to do when he was young?
2 What chore does the man especially hate doing?
3 What is the man doing while mopping the floor and vacuuming?

Questions 4 through 6 refer to the following conversation.

Man	Most people complain about doing chores ... but not you.
Woman	No, not at all. In fact, when I was young, I never minded doing chores. My mom and dad both worked and I kinda thought that

doing chores was like my special job. I liked to plan how I would do each one in the best way possible.

Man	And it really did turn into a job, didn't it?
Woman	That's right. When I got older, I started cleaning other people's houses—it was a part-time job for me. My first chores were things like making beds and mopping floors. A friend asked me to walk and feed her dog every day. I was too busy, but ...
Man	But you got someone to help you.
Woman	And that was the start of my business. Now my staff will do everything from feeding your cat to hanging up your clothes.

4 What did the woman NOT mind doing when she was young?
5 What did she start doing when she was older?
6 What will her staff do?

Questions 7 through 9 refer to the following conversation.

Friend	Hi, Rachel. What are you doing?
Rachel	Can't you see? I'm cleaning up! I have to take out the trash, hang up my clothes, and put away my CDs, and then I've—
Friend	What's the rush?
Rachel	My boyfriend's coming over and I said I'd mop the floor and do everything else.
Friend	So, you don't want to go to the movie tonight?
Rachel	I do! But I need to do all these chores first.
Friend	When is he coming over?
Rachel	Soon!
Friend	OK, OK. I'll help you.
Rachel	Oh! You're the best friend ever!
Friend	I know. Now, what do you want me to do first?
Rachel	Erm. Maybe you could start in the kitchen ... you know, mop the floor and put away the dishes?
Friend	Did you wash the dishes already?
Rachel	Yes, they're clean. And I'll vacuum the living room.
Friend	Great. We'll be done in no time.

7 What are the first three things Rachel says she has to do?
8 What does Rachel want her friend to do?
9 What is Rachel going to do while her friend is in the kitchen?

Go online!

Visit the *Sounds Good* website at **www.sounds-good-online.com**
Click on **Go online!** for extra listening practice.

Online listening

A 2 9 Listen for key details Eriko is talking to Ben about taking care of her place. Listen and check ☑ the picture that best describes Eriko's place.

B 2 9 Listen for specific information Listen again and check ☑ the things that Eriko asks Ben to do and the things that Ben says he did.

	The things Eriko asks Ben to do.	The things Ben says he did.
feed the pets	✔	
mop the floor		✔
take out the trash		✔
walk the dog	✔	
vacuum the living room		✔
wash the dishes		✔
water the plants	✔	✔

Download *Sounds Good* Podcast 28

Now listen to Podcast 28. You can do the activities, read the transcript, or simpy enjoy listening to young people from around the world.

33

Go online!

Students can visit the *Sounds Good* website at *www.sounds-good-online.com* and click on *Go online!* for extra listening practice based on the unit topic.

Online listening

This section can be used in two ways.

Students can use this for some optional, self-study listening practice outside the classroom. Students will see the same activity as printed in their Student Book and they will be able to complete it online, with immediate feedback on their answer choices.

Alternatively, you can use this section in class as an extension activity. The Online listening is recorded on the Class CDs for this purpose.

Students will listen to a phone conversation between Eriko and Ben. Eriko is asking her friend Ben to take care of her place while she is away. Ben has an Australian accent.

Audio script [CD2, track 9]

Eriko	Oh, Ben. Thanks so much for coming over. I didn't know who else to call! I completely forgot my cousin is getting married tomorrow. I'll just be gone for one night.
Ben	No problem, Eriko. So, you just want me to take care of your place?
Eriko	Yes, it really won't be any trouble. There's just Molly and Minnie.
Ben	Molly and Minnie?
Eriko	Yes, here's Molly. And there's Minnie over there. You should probably take Molly for a walk right away. And water the plants!
Ben	Uh, Eriko. I'm not so good with animals.
Eriko	Don't worry! They are the nicest pets! And don't forget to feed them. Gotta run!

The next day.

Eriko	Hello, I'm home! Molly! Minnie! How are you? Hello, Ben. Oh, Ben, what happened to your hand?
Ben	Molly bit me.
Eriko	Why? What did you do?
Ben	I was taking out the trash and Molly bit the bag and tore it open. There was trash and broken glass all over the place.
Eriko	Broken glass?
Ben	Yes. I was washing the dishes and Minnie knocked over a couple of glasses.
Eriko	Oh!
Ben	I tried to clean up, but when I mopped the floor, Molly bit me.
Eriko	Yes, Molly doesn't like the mop. I should have told you. Did you water the plants?
Ben	Yes ... until Minnie knocked them over.
Eriko	She did what?
Ben	Don't worry. I vacuumed it all up.
Eriko	Well, I'm so sorry, Ben. I'm sure they'll be better next time.
Ben	Eriko, believe me. There won't be a next time.

 Podcast 28

Encourage students to download Podcast 28. Inspired by the unit topic, it is authentic and high-interest, and features young people from around the world.

5

Let's do something fun!

Goals
- Identifying leisure activities
- Understanding entertainment options

Learn the language

A **2** **10** **What do you like to do on Saturday night? Look at the pictures and complete the phrases with the words from the box. Then listen and number the pictures.**

> band   comedy   festival   magic   online   play   karaoke   tickets

6

5

8

7

go to ___*karaoke*___

see a ___*magic*___ show

watch a ___*play*___

book tickets ___*online*___

2

1

4

3

go to the Arts ___*Festival*___

catch a ___*band*___

buy ___*tickets*___ at the door

check out a ___*comedy*___ show

FOCUS

B **2** **11** **Listen and write the letter to match each sentence with the correct response.**

1 What are you up to this weekend?   _F_

2 Do you feel like going clubbing?   _C_

3 I wouldn't mind going to a concert.   _E_

4 What else looks interesting?   _A_

5 Let's go see that new DJ tonight.   _D_

6 What do we do about tickets?   _B_

A Look, this one is a comedy show. Could be good.

B We can book them in advance or buy them at the door.

C I'm not really into clubbing.

D OK, I'm sold.

E I'll pass. I'm really not in the mood for a concert.

F I don't know. Let's do something fun.

34

Unit overview

The topic of this unit is leisure activities. In Listening task one, students will listen to Brad and Hae-Jin, who are trying to decide what to do this weekend and talking about the different events at an arts festival. In Listening task two, students will listen to six conversations in different contexts. In the speaking activities, students will have an opportunity to talk about their leisure activities and find an activity their group members would like to do together.

Learn the language

- Ask students what they like to do on Saturday night. Ask them what sorts of leisure activities they do regularly and which they do only occasionally.

- Have students open the book and look at the pictures. Ask them what the people are doing in each picture.

- Read the words in the box and ask students to complete the phrases with the words based on what they see in the pictures.

- Allow students a few minutes to finish writing the answers.

- Play the audio (CD2, track 10) and have students number the pictures.

- Review the answers with students by playing the audio again. Stop the CD and play each sentence again as often as necessary.

Audio script [CD2, track 10]

1   Catch a band. Let's catch a band on Friday night.
2   Go to the Arts Festival. I'm going to the Arts Festival next week.
3   Check out a comedy show. Let's check out a comedy show tomorrow night.
4   Buy tickets at the door. Let's wait and buy tickets at the door.
5   See a magic show. I'm going to see a magic show.
6   Go to karaoke. We can go to karaoke on Saturday night.
7   Book tickets online. We can book tickets online.
8   Watch a play. Let's watch a play tomorrow night.

B

- Say the questions and statements in the *Focus* box to elicit some possible responses from students.

- Have students read through the sentences to get an idea of what they will be listening for.

- Play the audio (CD2, track 11) and have students match the sentences.

- Review the answers by playing the audio again.

- Have students role-play the sentences and responses in the *Focus* box.

Language note

When someone says *I'm sold*, he/she means that he/she agrees or thinks something is a good idea.

People can *catch* a show, a play, a concert or something that they watch, but *go* to karaoke, a dance or something that they are actively involved in as participants.

Audio script [CD2, track 11]

1
Woman   What are you up to this weekend?
Man   I don't know. Let's do something fun.

2
Woman   Do you feel like going clubbing?
Man   I'm not really into clubbing.

3
Woman   I wouldn't mind going to a concert.
Man   I'll pass. I'm really not in the mood for a concert.

4
Woman   What else looks interesting?
Man   Look, this one is a comedy show. Could be good.

5
Woman   Let's go see that new DJ tonight.
Man   OK, I'm sold.

6
Woman   What do we do about tickets?
Man   We can book them in advance or buy them at the door.

Listening task one

A **2** **12** Listen for gist **What are Brad and Hae-Jin talking about? Listen and choose the best answer.**

A going dancing   **B** a hip-hop concert   **C** what to do this weekend

B **2** **13** Listen for feelings **Brad and Hae-Jin feel differently about what they would like to do this weekend. Listen and write B next to what Brad likes and H next to what Hae-Jin likes. Check ☑ the thing that they decide to do.**

C **2** **13** Listen for specific information **Listen again and choose the best answer to each question.**

1 Why does Brad say they are in luck?

   (**A**) The Arts Festival is on this weekend.
   B Hae-Jin likes to watch plays.
   C He has tickets for one of the Arts Festival shows.

2 What is Hae-Jin NOT in the mood for?

   A Dinner.
   (**B**) A play.
   C Clubbing.

3 What does Brad say looks interesting?

   A A couple of singers.
   B One of the concerts.
   (**C**) A couple of the movies.

4 What would Hae-Jin NOT mind seeing?

   (**A**) A comedy show.
   B A concert.
   C The schedule.

Speak out!

Work with a partner. Look at the above advertisements and think about what you would and wouldn't like to do. Discuss with your partner and try to decide what things you would both like to do.

Use the language in **FOCUS** to help you.

35

Listening task one

- Introduce the characters Brad and Hae-Jin. Tell students that Brad has a Canadian accent. Students need to decide what they are talking about.

- Play the audio (CD2, track 12) and have students choose the best answer.

- Review the answers with students. What did they hear that helped them decide?

Audio script [CD2, track 12]

Hae-Jin So, Brad. What are you up to this weekend?

Brad I don't know. What do you feel like doing? Do you want to catch a band? Perhaps the Red Beats concert?

Hae-Jin Oh, no. I'm not really into hip-hop … perhaps we can just hang out …

Brad Oh, come on, Hae-Jin! It's Saturday night. Let's do something fun. Do you want to go dancing? We could go to a club.

- Brad and Hae-Jin feel differently about the entertainment options at the Arts Festival. Tell students to listen carefully to decide what events each of them likes.

- Have students look at the pictures and say what event is shown in each of the pictures.

- Play the audio (CD2, track 13) and have students write the letters and check the appropriate box.

- Review the answers with students.

Audio script [CD2, track 13]

Brad We're in luck. The Arts Festival is on this weekend.

Hae-Jin The Arts Festival? Oh, yeah … lots of concerts and plays … just what I feel like.

Brad Oh, come on. I know you're not really into plays, but give them a chance. We went to that Shakespeare play last year, remember? It was great!

Hae-Jin Sorry. I'm really not in the mood for a play.

Brad Well, there are movies too. Look. Here's the schedule. Uh, what do you feel like seeing?

Hae-Jin I don't know. What looks good?

Brad A couple of the movies look interesting. Mm … what about this one: *Motorcycles*

in the Mud. It's about two friends who take a motorcycle trip across India during the rainy season.

Hae-Jin Sounds like a guy film. I'll pass. What else looks interesting? Are there any comedy acts? I wouldn't mind seeing a comedy show. Or look, this one here is a magic show. A magic show could be good.

Brad No one's into stupid magic shows.

Hae-Jin Oh … actually, it's already sold out. Hey, feel like going clubbing? Look at this one. There's this famous DJ playing really cool music at a club on Smith Street.

Brad OK. I'm sold. When does it start?

Hae-Jin Mm … doors open at nine p.m.

Brad What do we do about tickets?

Hae-Jin Um, let's see. We'll just go and buy them at the door.

- Put students into pairs and have them read through the sentences and discuss possible answers to each question.

- Play audio (CD2, track 13) again and have students choose the best answers.

- Review the answers with students.

Speak out!

- Review the language in the *Focus* box on the previous Student Book page.

- Put students into pairs and explain the speaking activity.

- Encourage students to give reasons why they would prefer one activity over another.

Model conversation

A Do you feel like going clubbing?

B No. I'm not really into clubbing.

A What else looks interesting?

B Maybe this comedy show.

A OK, I'm sold.

Extension

Put students into pairs and have one partner pretend that he or she is working at a ticket office and the other person is trying to book tickets. Many of the shows are sold out or the tickets are too expensive. Students need to negotiate to get tickets for something they want to see.

Unit **5**

Listening task two

A **2** **14-19** Listen for context Look at the pictures. Where are these people? Listen and number the pictures.

3

1

6

2

5

4

B **2** **14-19** Listen for implied intention Listen again and choose the best answer to each question.

1 Why does the woman want to go clubbing?

  A She hasn't been clubbing for a long time.
  (B) She likes the music the DJ is playing at the club.
  C The club is very small.

2 Why are the people buying tickets?

  A To see a movie at 6:30.
  (B) To see a movie at 7:30.
  C To see a concert.

3 Why is Connie singing?

  (A) She loves karaoke.
  B She sounds good.
  C She is really good at singing.

4 Why is the woman worried?

  A She doesn't want to miss the warm-up band.
  (B) She doesn't want to miss any of the songs.
  C The stadium is too big and she can't see the band.

5 Why is the waiter surprised?

  (A) Four more people turned up.
  B The people do not have a reservation.
  C The people want to sit outside.

6 Why do the two friends need a blanket?

  A They might fall asleep if their team is losing.
  (B) They might feel cold.
  C They need to sit at a table outside.

Speak out!

2 **14-19** Work with a partner. Listen again and write a list of key words that help you identify each place. Brainstorm other words and phrases that make you think of each place.

36

Listening task two

- The new language introduced in this section includes the following phrases and sentences:

    She sounds terrible!
    it's just the warm-up act
    Do you have reservations?
    we may need to put two of you at the bar
    Just kidding.

- Have students look at the pictures and say what the people are doing in each picture. Do any of the students do these leisure activities?

- Explain that students will listen to six conversations and they need to use the context clues to decide where the speakers are.

- Play the audio (CD2, tracks 14–19) and have students number the pictures. Point out that the man and woman in Conversation 1 are Brad and Hae-Jin from Listening task one; the woman in Conversation 2 has a Canadian accent; in Conversation 3, the first man has a British accent and the second man has an Australian accent; in Conversation 4, the woman has a Canadian accent and the man has an Australian accent; in Conversation 6, the second man has a Canadian accent.

- Ask students what the people are actually doing to review the answers, e.g., *The people in Conversation 1 are talking about buying tickets to see a famous DJ at a club.*

Audio script [CD2, tracks 14–19]

1

Hae-Jin Did you get the tickets?

Brad I did, but they were really expensive. He's such a famous DJ and it's a pretty small club. There weren't many tickets left.

Hae-Jin Yeah, I was afraid of that, but I really love his music.

2

Man Good evening. How can I help you?

Woman Yes, we'd like two tickets for the seven thirty show.

Man That'll be seventeen dollars.

Woman OK. Here you are.

Man And here are your tickets. Go right in, it's the third door to your left, just past the popcorn and drinks.

Woman Thanks.

3

Man 1 Excuse me, we're looking for our friends …

Woman Oh, yeah, they're in room fifteen.

Man 2 Thanks a lot. I think I can hear Connie singing.

Man 1 She sounds terrible!

Man 2 Shh! I know, but she really loves it. And she thinks she's really good.

4

Woman Hurry up, Glen. I can hear them. It's already started.

Man Don't worry … it's just the warm-up act.

Woman OK, but let's run. The stadium is so big, and I don't want to miss the first song.

5

Man Good evening. Do you have reservations?

Woman Yes, we do. The last name is Johnson. Uh … we asked for a table for four but now we have four extra people. Is that OK?

Man Four more?! I'm sure it's no problem, but we may need to put two of you at the bar and two at the table outside.

Woman What!?

Man Just kidding.

6

Man 1 OK, did you bring a blanket? It might be cold.

Man 2 Yeah, I've got a blanket and a small umbrella in my bag. It might rain.

Man 1 Great, but if our team is losing, I'm leaving.

Man 2 What? Are you serious?

B

- Have students read through the questions and answer choices.

- Play the audio (CD2, tracks 14–19) again and have students choose the best answers.

- Review the answers with students.

Speak out!

- The aim of this section is to integrate listening with other skills. In this case, students write a list of words before verbally brainstorming.

- Put students into pairs and explain the speaking activity.

- Play the audio (CD2, tracks 14–19) once more and have students write down the key words.

- Have pairs work together to brainstorm other words and phrases that make them think of each place.

- Have some pairs read out their key words.

Write what you hear

A **2 20** When we talk, we often use contractions and reductions. We pronounce two short words together as if they are one word. Listen and complete the sentences.

Example: (Didya get the tickets?) ➞ _____*Did you*_____ get the tickets?

1 _____*We're in*_____ luck.
2 _____*Here's the*_____ schedule.
3 _____*What do you*_____ feel like seeing?
4 I _____*don't know*_____ .
5 _____*What about*_____ this one?
6 _____*Are there any*_____ comedy acts?
7 _____*We'll just go*_____ and _____*buy them at*_____ the door.
8 _____*When does it start?*_____

B **2 20** Now listen again and repeat. Try saying the contractions and reductions smoothly, pronouncing the words together as if they are one word.

Use what you learn

A What do you do for fun? Make a list of different activities you do for fun in your free time. (*Answers may vary.*)

Things I do for fun in my free time
– *hang out with friends*
– *go to the gym*
– *read*
– *go to the movies*
– *go to karaoke*
– *play soccer*

B Work in groups of three. Ask questions to find other people who want to do the same things as you.

A Do you want to go to the movies?
B No, thanks. I don't like movies.
C How about going to a club?
A No, I'm not into clubbing.
B Let's see a play then.
C OK.

37

Write what you hear

Aim

The aim of this section is for students to identify and pronounce words in some common contractions and reductions.

In contractions and reductions, short function words join together to be pronounced as one word. Contractions have a standard written form. However, reductions are not usually written as one word, although non-standard spellings are sometimes used.

Contractions		Reductions	
He is ➜	*He's*	Did you ➜	*Didya*
Here is ➜	*Here's*	don't know ➜	*dunno*
We are ➜	*We're*	What about … ➜	*Whaddabout*
We will ➜	*We'll*	When does it ➜	*When duzzit*

The word *don't* is a contraction of *do + not*. However, it is often joined with the following word *know* and pronounced as *dunno*.

- Introduce the topic of contractions and reductions and explain their difference.
- Point out the example and model the sentence.
- Play the audio (CD2, track 20) and have students fill in the gaps with either contractions or the full written forms of reductions.
- Review the answers with students by playing the audio again. Encourage students to find and correct any of their mistakes.

Audio script [CD2, track 20]

Example: Did you get the tickets?
1   We're in luck.
2   Here's the schedule.
3   What do you feel like seeing?
4   I don't know.
5   What about this one?
6   Are there any comedy acts?
7   We'll just go and buy them at the door.
8   When does it start?

- Play the audio (CD2, track 20) again. This time, ask students to repeat each sentence out loud, paying special attention to the contractions and reductions.
- Monitor and provide feedback on students' pronunciation. Model the correct pronunciation if necessary.

Use what you learn

Aim

The aim of this section is to give students the opportunity to talk about their leisure activities.

- Review the unit vocabulary and functional language by asking students what activities they have done for fun recently.
- Have students work individually to write their own list of fun activities.

B

- Explain the activity and model the sentences at the bottom of the page with two students.
- Put students into groups of three and have them work together to complete the activity. Encourage groups to talk about the activities not mentioned in the unit.

Extension

Using the board, do a whole-class survey. Make a list of the most and the least popular activities in the class.

Unit 5

Your score:

_____ /12

Test yourself

2 21 You will hear a talk about Mike's job. You will have to answer ten questions of different kinds. First, read through all the questions. Then listen and answer the questions.

Question 1. Choose THREE letters A–G.

1 Which of the following does Mike mention?

A Magic shows.
(B) Concerts.
(C) Plays.
D Art galleries.

E Sports events.
(F) Movies.
G Karaoke.

Questions 2 and 3. Choose the correct letter, A, B or C.

2 What is Mike's job?

A He is an entertainer.
(B) He is an entertainment reporter.
C He works for the Arts Festival.

3 Which of the following does Mike NOT have to do?

A Write about movies.
(B) Watch the whole movie or play.
C Bring a friend.

Questions 4–7. Complete the table below. Write NO MORE THAN THREE WORDS for each answer.

Mike doesn't …	Mike goes to many …	Mike looks at …
have to book (4) _tickets online_ .	premieres of (6) _movies_ .	two or more things a night.
buy tickets (5) _at the door_ .	concerts.	five or more shows a day.
have to stay for the whole show.	plays.	the (7) _Arts Festival schedule_ for weeks.

Questions 8–10. Complete the sentences below. Write NO MORE THAN THREE WORDS for each answer.

8 If a movie is bad, Mike will leave and go _____ _to another event_ .

9 If a comedian makes fun of him, Mike doesn't mind because it's part _____ _of his job_ .

10 Mike thinks most people will stay for a whole movie or play, even if _____ _it's not good_ .

38

Test yourself

Aim

The aim of this section is to provide exam practice. Students will listen to a talk and then answer ten questions of different kinds. The questions are not recorded on the audio.

Explain the test format. Students should read the questions and answer choices first so they have a general idea of the types of information they will listen for. While listening to the talk, students may take notes of any key points to help them answer the questions. Explain that in questions 4–10 where students are required to complete sentences, apart from giving the correct information, their answers should also fit into the sentences grammatically.

Point out that Mike, the man doing the talk, has a British accent.

Audio script [CD2, track 21]

Mike My name's Mike and people think I have a wonderful job and I guess I have to agree. I never have to book tickets online and I don't even have to buy tickets at the door. I'm the entertainment reporter for *Max Magazine*. What does it mean? It means I get invitations and free tickets to more parties, movies, plays and concerts that I can go to. Often, I go to two or more things a night—especially if the first one is terrible. I have to go to a lot of premieres of movies that I don't really like, but I only have to sit there long enough to see if they're good or bad. If they're bad, I'll leave and go to another event. If it looks interesting, I'll stay. The same is true of plays and concerts.

The time of year that is really busy for me is the Arts Festival. I look at the schedule for weeks to try to decide what to see. Then I go to five or more shows a day. A lot of people know that I write for *Max Magazine* so when I see a comedy show, the guy on stage will often make fun of me. It's OK, it's part of his job and I think it's funny.

Sometimes I take friends to a show, but only if I know it's going to be good. Otherwise, I might want to leave and my friend might want to stay. Most people want to stay for a whole movie or play, even if it's not good.

Go online!

Visit the *Sounds Good* website at **www.sounds-good-online.com**
Click on **Go online!** for extra listening practice.

Online listening

A **2 22** [Listen for key details] Jason is trying to convince his friend Sally to go out. Which activities does he suggest doing? Listen and check ☑ the correct pictures.

B **2 22** [Listen for attitudes] Listen again and choose the best answers.

1 When Jason drops by, Sally is ...

    A angry that he is late.
    (B) annoyed to see him.
    C happy he has come over.

2 Jason ...

    A wants to go see a play.
    B can't stand clubbing.
    (C) likes clubbing.

3 Sally says she doesn't want to go to a movie because ...

    A she always eats too much popcorn.
    B she's going to see a movie tomorrow.
    (C) she hates the smell of popcorn.

4 Sally says she doesn't want to see the Rebel Rockets because ...

    (A) she can't stand loud music.
    B there are probably no tickets at the door.
    C it is probably too late to buy tickets.

5 Jason thinks Sally ...

    (A) really does want to go out with him.
    B is trying to get rid of him.
    C is going to be busy that night.

6 The real reason Sally doesn't want to go out with Jason is ...

    A that she has to go to the doctor.
    (B) that she is going out with someone else.
    C that she already went out every night this week.

Download *Sounds Good* Podcast 29

Now listen to Podcast 29. You can do the activities, read the transcript, or simpy enjoy listening to young people from around the world.

Go online!

Students can visit the *Sounds Good* website at *www.sounds-good-online.com* and click on *Go online!* for extra listening practice based on the unit topic.

Online listening

This section can be used in two ways.

Students can use this for some optional, self-study listening practice outside the classroom. Students will see the same activity as printed in their Student Book and they will be able to complete it online, with immediate feedback on their answer choices.

Alternatively, you can use this section in class as an extension activity. The Online listening is recorded on the Class CDs for this purpose.

Students will listen to a conversation between Sally and her friend Jason. Jason is trying to convince Sally to go out, but Sally has many reasons why she does not want to go. Students will finally find out the real reason: Sally has a date with another man. He has a British accent.

Audio script [CD2, track 22]

Sally Jason … uh, what are you doing here?

Jason Surprise, Sally! I was in the neighborhood. I know you said you didn't want to do anything tonight, but I thought I'd stop by. So, what are you up to tonight?

Sally Uh, nothing. I, uh, I really don't feel like going out.

Jason Oh, come on. It'll be fun. Look, I've got the latest entertainment magazine. There must be something you want to do.

Sally But, I already said—

Jason Nice try, but I won't take no for an answer. You're gonna have fun! Look here, The Purple Star. You've heard of it, haven't you? It's a new club. Feel like clubbing?

Sally No, Jason. I'm not really into clubbing. Actually—

Jason Doesn't matter! There are lots of other things. A movie? There's a new movie about—

Sally I can't stand the smell of popcorn.

Jason OK, then. But you can't stay home by yourself! I mean … what else looks interesting? I know, let's go see a band. The Rebel Rockets are playing. As for tickets, I'm sure we can buy them at the door.

Sally No, they're too loud. Maybe you better just go with some other friends.

Jason OK. Well, you must be hungry. I bet we can get reservations at Tsukiji, the sushi place.

Sally You know, Jason. I don't feel well. I think you better just go now.

(doorbell rings)

Sally Erm …

Jason Wasn't that your doorbell?

Sally Uh, yeah.

Jason And … aren't you gonna see who's there?

Sally I guess so.

Man Hi, Sally. Sorry I'm late. Are you ready to go? I made reservations at Tsukiji, the new Japanese restaurant, and I've got tickets to the movie you wanted to see.

Podcast 29

Encourage students to download Podcast 29. Inspired by the unit topic, it is authentic and high-interest, and features young people from around the world.

6 Enjoy your stay.

Goals
• Understanding air travel
• Identifying hotel and travel options

Learn the language

A **2** **23** Do you like traveling? Have you ever been on a plane? Match the words to the things in the pictures. Listen and check your answers.

1 boarding pass   **2** flight attendant   **3** aisle seat   **4** overhead compartment

5 carry-on bag   **6** seatbelt   **7** take-off   **8** seatback table   **9** arrival card   **10** landing

FOCUS

B **2** **24** Listen and fill in the blanks using the words above.

1 How many bags will you be checking?

None. I just have one _____carry-on bag_____.

2 May I see your _____boarding pass_____, please?

Here you are. Do I need to fill out an _____arrival card_____?

3 Please put your briefcase in the _____overhead compartment_____.

4 We're getting ready for _____take-off_____.

Please fasten your _____seatbelt_____.

5 We're getting ready for _____landing_____. Please put your _____seatback table_____ away.

40

Unit overview

The topic of this unit is travel. In Listening task one, students will listen to some people talking at an airport or on a plane. In Listening task two, students will listen to two friends making arrangements for transportation and a place to stay. In the speaking activities, students will have an opportunity to role-play the conversations at different scenes on a trip.

Learn the language

- Ask students whether they like traveling. Have they ever been on a plane? What are the names for the different places at an airport? What are the steps they take at an airport before they get on the plane?

- Have students open the book and look at the pictures. Ask them what is shown in each picture.

- Read the words (1–10) and ask students to match them to the things in the pictures.

- Allow students a few minutes to finish writing the answers.

- Play the audio (CD2, track 23) and have students check their answers. Stop the CD and play each sentence again as often as necessary.

- Review the words for parts of an airplane and other airline terminology.

Audio script [CD2, track 23]

1 Boarding pass. Please show me your boarding pass.
2 Flight attendant. He works as a flight attendant.
3 Aisle seat. Seat 33C is an aisle seat.
4 Overhead compartment. Put your bag in the overhead compartment.
5 Carry-on bag. Put your carry-on bag in the overhead compartment.
6 Seatbelt. Please fasten your seatbelt.
7 Take-off. We're ready for take-off.
8 Seatback table. Put your seatback table down.
9 Arrival card. Every visitor must fill out an arrival card.
10 Landing. We're ready for landing.

B

- Ask students the two questions in the *Focus* box to elicit some possible responses.

- Have students read through the sentences to get an idea of what they will be listening for.

- Play the audio (CD2, track 24) and have students fill in the missing words.

- Review the answers by playing the audio again.

Audio script [CD2, track 24]

1
Man	How many bags will you be checking?
Woman	None. I just have one carry-on bag.

2
Woman	May I see your boarding pass, please?
Man	Here you are. Do I need to fill out an arrival card?

3
Woman	Please put your briefcase in the overhead compartment.

4
Man	We are getting ready for take-off. Please fasten your seatbelt.

5
Woman	We're getting ready for landing. Please put your seatback table away.

Listening task one

 25-29 Listen for context **Look at the pictures. Where are these people? Listen and number the pictures.**

B **2** **25-29** Listen for cause and effect **Listen again and choose the best answers.**

1 The passenger gets seat 32B because ...

   A he asked for an aisle seat.
   B there are no aisle seats left.

2 The passenger needs to put his briefcase under the seat because ...

   A he cannot reach the overhead compartment.
   B the overhead compartment is full.

3 The passenger has chicken because ...

   A he does not like fish or pasta.
   B there is no more fish.

4 The pilot asks the passengers to put the seatback tables away because ...

   A the plane is on its final descent.
   B it is time for take-off.

5 The passenger talks about visiting friends because ...

   A he is asked the purpose of his trip.
   B he is really on a business trip.

Speak out!

Work with a partner. Pretend you are a passenger and your partner is working at an airport. Give instructions and ask questions. Take turns.

Use the language in **FOCUS** to help you.

41

Listening task one

- Have students look at the pictures and say where the people in each picture are and what is going on in each picture.

- Play the audio (CD2, tracks 25–29) and have students number the pictures. Point out that the man in Conversation 1 on track 25 and the woman in Conversation 2 on track 26 have Australian accents; the woman in Conversation 3 on track 27 has a Canadian accent; the man in Conversation 5 has a Japanese accent.

- Review the answers with students.

- Ask students which words and phrases helped them decide the picture for each conversation.

Audio script [CD2, tracks 25–29]

1

Woman	Good morning. May I see your ticket and passport, please?
Man	Here you are. And, could I get an aisle seat?
Woman	Mm … let me see. Uh, yes. No problem. Seat 32B.
Man	Thanks.
Woman	How many bags are you checking?
Man	Just one. And I have one carry-on bag.
Woman	Fine. Here's your boarding pass.

2

Woman	Excuse me, sir. You can't leave your briefcase on the seat.
Man	But the overhead compartment is full.
Woman	Then you have to put it under the seat in front of you.

3

Woman	Would you like the chicken or the fish for lunch?
Man	The fish, please.
Woman	OK, oh … Mm, let me check with the other flight attendant. Sally, any more fish? No? Sorry, sir. We're out of the fish.
Man	OK. Chicken, then.
Woman	And what would you like to drink?

4

Man	We've begun our final descent into San Francisco. In preparation for landing, please put the seatback tables away, return your seats to their upright position and make sure your seatbelt is securely fastened.

5

Woman	Welcome to the United States. Passport and arrival card, please.
Man	Here you are.
Woman	Where are you coming from today, sir?
Man	Osaka, Japan.
Woman	And you're going … ?
Man	Uh, to Dallas, Texas.
Woman	And the purpose of your visit?
Man	Just visiting friends.
Woman	Staying with friends then, huh? How long?
Man	Two weeks.
Woman	Enjoy your stay. Next!

B

- Ask students to listen again to find out the reason why certain things happen in each conversation.

- Have students read through the sentences and the answer choices.

- Play the audio (CD2, tracks 25–29) again and have students choose the best answers.

- Review the answers with students.

Speak out!

- Review the language in the *Focus* box on the previous Student Book page.

- Put students into pairs and explain the speaking activity.

- Encourage students to play different roles.

Model conversation

A How many bags are you checking?
B None. I just have one carry-on bag.
A Fine. Here's your boarding pass.
B Thanks.

Unit 6

Listening task two

A **2** **30-32** Listen for key details) Two friends are making arrangements for a place to stay. Look at the three sets of pictures. Listen and check ☑ the correct picture for each question.

1 Where do they decide to stay?

2 How do they decide to get to town?

3 Which room are they going to stay in?

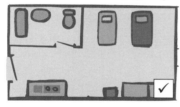  

B **2** **30-32** Listen for specific information) **Listen again and choose the best answers.**

1 The two friends decide to get the train because ...

   A it is the cheapest.
   B they have just missed the shuttle bus.
   C they do not want to wait for a taxi.

2 Each train ticket to get into town costs ...

   A $16
   B $6
   C $8

3 The two friends are surprised to find ...

   A the pool is on the same floor as their room.
   B the pool is on the second floor.
   C the pool is closed.

Speak out!

2 **30-32**) Work with a partner. Listen again. How do you think the conversation would continue once they hear the pool is closed? Discuss with your partner and write four more lines of conversation. Read them out to the class.

42

Listening task two

- The new language introduced in this section includes the following words, phrases and sentences:

luxury hotel	room with twin beds
budget hotel	How do we get into town?
youth hostel	kitchenette
just fill in the form	

- Have students look at the pictures and say what is shown in each picture.

- Explain that students will listen to three conversations in which two friends, who have just arrived in a new place, are making arrangements for transportation and a place to stay. The two friends both have Canadian accents.

- Play the audio (CD2, tracks 30–32) and have students check the correct picture for each conversation.

- Ask students which words or phrases helped them decide the picture for each conversation.

Audio script [CD2, tracks 30–32]

1

Man 1	Hi, we'd like to book a place downtown, not too expensive.
Woman	A luxury hotel, budget hotel, youth hostel … ?
Man 2	A reasonable hotel—with a pool? We want a pool.
Woman	Sure. There's The Crown, a nice budget hotel close to everything.
Man 1	Good. A room with twin beds for five nights?
Woman	OK … sixty-eight dollars per night including breakfast.
Man 2	That's fine.

2

Man 1	How do we get into town?
Woman	You can take a hotel shuttle bus, a taxi or a train.
Man 2	Which is the cheapest?
Woman	The shuttle bus, but it's not the fastest. It has ten stops before your hotel.
Man 1	When's the next one?
Woman	You just missed it. The next one's in an hour.
Man 2	We can't wait for a whole hour. Let's take the train. Uh, we don't have to wait an hour for the train, do we?
Woman	No. It's every ten minutes and only takes thirty minutes.
Man 2	And we get tickets … ?
Woman	Here. Two tickets, Central Station … Here you are. Sixteen dollars.
Man 1	I'll get that.

Woman	It's a two-minute walk from the station to your hotel. Here's a map.
Man 2	And we catch the train … ?
Woman	Around the corner. The next train leaves in … three minutes.

3

Man 1	Hi, check in, please.
Woman	Certainly. Do you have a reservation?
Man 1	Yes, it's under Maguire.
Woman	Mm. Here it is. Twin beds and a kitchenette?
Man 1	No. We didn't ask for a kitchenette.
Woman	It's the same price with or without one.
Man 1	Oh, OK.
Woman	OK, just fill in the form and I'll get your key.
Man 1	OK.
Woman	So, seventh floor, room seven-oh-three. Take the elevator behind you. The café has breakfast from seven to ten, and there's a laundromat on the second floor.
Man 1	Second floor … thanks.
Man 2	And, where's the swimming pool?
Woman	Third floor … but I'm afraid the pool is closed this week.
Man 2	Oh, you're kidding!

- Have students read through the sentences and the answer choices.

- Play the audio (CD2, tracks 30–32) again and have students choose the best answers.

- Review the answers with students. If necessary, play the audio again.

Speak out!

- The aim of this section is to integrate listening with other skills. In this case, students write lines of dialogue before presenting to the class.

- Put students into pairs and explain the speaking activity.

- Play the audio (CD2, tracks 30–32) once more. Have pairs discuss how the conversation would continue and write four more lines for the conversation.

- Have some pairs role-play their lines to the class.

Model conversation

A Do you want to try another hotel?
B Sure. Maybe the woman at the desk could recommend something close by.
A But are you sure a pool is important? Maybe there's a public pool near here.
B OK, let's ask first.

Write what you hear

A **2 33** Can you hear the difference between the sounds /r/ and /l/? At the end of words, /r/ and /l/ are sometimes difficult to hear because they often link to the sound that follows. Listen and complete the sentences.

Example: (Could I get an aisle seat?) ➡ Could I get an ____*aisle seat*____?

1 Would you like the chicken ____*or the*____ fish ____*for lunch*____?

2 Passport and ____*arrival card*____ please.

3 We've begun ____*our final descent into*____ San Francisco.

4 Make ____*sure your seatbelt*____ is securely fastened.

5 You can take a ____*hotel shuttle bus*____.

6 I'm afraid ____*the pool is closed*____ this week.

7 Just ____*fill in the*____ form and ____*I'll get your key*____.

8 ____*We can't wait for a whole hour.*____

B **2 33** Now listen again and repeat. Try saying the sentences as naturally as possible.

Use what you learn

A Imagine you are going on a trip. Make a list of the different things you would need to do or choose. (Answers may vary.)

Scene	Question	Answer
At the airport check-in	seat?	*a window seat*
	how many bags?	*two suitcases*
On the plane	drink?	*a tomato juice*
	food?	*the fish*
At the information desk	transportation?	*the train*
	accommodation?	*a luxury hotel*

B Work in pairs. Imagine you are going on a trip. With your partner, role-play the three different scenes. Take turns.

A Could I get a window seat?
B No problem. Seat 43A. How many bags are you checking?
A Two suitcases. I also have one carry-on bag.

43

Write what you hear

Aim

The aim of this section is for students to distinguish between and correctly pronounce the sounds /r/ and /l/ at the end of words in connected speech.

The sounds /r/ and /l/ are made by using the tip of the tongue. The difference between them involves the tooth ridge, which is just behind the upper front teeth. When making the /r/ sound, the tongue tip does not touch the tooth ridge and is curled upwards. When making the /l/ sound, the tongue tip touches the tooth ridge.

When /r/ and /l/ appear at the end of words, they often link to the sound that follows. In such cases, you may not hear the /r/ or /l/ sound clearly, but the sound formed by linking /r/ or /l/ to the sound that follows. For example, *fill in the form* sounds like /fɪlɪn/ *the form*. *Wait for a whole week* sounds like *wait* /fɔːrə/ *whole week*.

- Introduce the topic of the /r/ and /l/ sounds. Review the pronunciation of the two sounds to make sure that students understand the difference between the two sounds.
- Point out the example and model the sentence.
- Play the audio (CD2, track 33) and have students fill in the missing words.
- Have some students write their answers on the board. Play the audio again. Encourage students to find and correct any of their mistakes.

Audio script [CD2, track 33]

Example: Could I get an aisle seat?
1   Would you like the chicken or the fish for lunch?
2   Passport and arrival card please.
3   We've begun our final descent into San Francisco.
4   Make sure your seatbelt is securely fastened.
5   You can take a hotel shuttle bus.
6   I'm afraid the pool is closed this week.
7   Just fill in the form and I'll get your key.
8   We can't wait for a whole hour.

- Play the audio (CD2, track 33) again. This time, ask students to repeat each sentence out loud, paying special attention to the pronunciation of the /r/ and /l/ sounds.
- Monitor and provide feedback on students' pronunciation.

Use what you learn

Aim

The aim of this section is to give students the opportunity to role-play the conversations at different scenes on a trip.

- Review the unit vocabulary and functional language by pretending to be a traveler and asking students for information about flights, transportation and hotels.
- Have students work individually to fill in the table with the things they need to do or choose in preparation for the role-play.

B

- Explain the activity and model the sentences at the bottom of the page with a student.
- Put students into pairs and have them role-play the conversations at three different scenes on a trip.
- Have some pairs role-play their scenes to the rest of the class.

Unit **6**

Test yourself

2 (34) For each question, you will hear four statements about a picture. The statements are not printed in your book. Choose the statement that best describes what you see in the picture.

1

(A) B C D

4

A B (C) D

2

A (B) C D

5

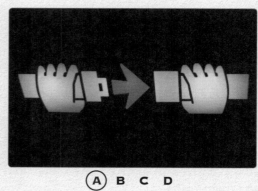

(A) B C D

3

A (B) C D

6

A B (C) D

Test yourself

Aim

The aim of this section is to provide exam practice. For each question, students will listen to four short statements about a picture and choose the statement that best describes what they see in the picture.

Explain the test format. Students will have seven seconds after each question to choose the best statement. Students should look at the pictures first and mentally summarize the picture, so they can predict what will be said. The four statements might be quite similar, so students need to listen to all the statements to make sure they get the details correct.

Audio script [CD2, track 34]

1.   **A** The people are waiting to check in.
     B The people are boarding the plane.
     C The people are shopping.
     D The people are checking the schedule.

2.   **A** The man is sitting on the plane.
     B The man is waiting at the airport.
     C The man is watching television.
     D The man is talking to his friends.

3.   **A** The seatback table is down.
     B The seatback table is up.
     C The table is in the airport.
     D The table is for tea.

4.   **A** He is on the plane.
     B He is checking in his suitcase.
     C He has one suitcase and one carry-on bag.
     D He is carrying a box.

5.   **A** The sign says to fasten your seatbelt.
     B The sign is in the airport restaurant.
     C The sign says to return to your seat.
     D The sign is in an office at the airport.

6.   **A** She's sitting in the aisle seat.
     B She's looking out the window.
     C She's sitting in the window seat.
     D She's reading a magazine.

Go online!

Visit the *Sounds Good* website at ***www.sounds-good-online.com***
Click on ***Go online!*** for extra listening practice.

Online listening

A **2** **35** Listen for specific information Listen to an airport worker talking about some of the things he has seen and heard. Complete the table below with the things passengers forget, leave behind at the airport or try to take on the plane.

Forget	Leave behind	Try to take on the plane
passports	*bags of shopping*	*dogs*
to get a visa	*computers*	
tickets	*guitars*	
	snowboards	

B **2** **35** Listen for specific information Listen again and circle T for True or F for False.

1 People get upset when they forget their passports.　　(T)　F
2 It is a big problem if you forget your ticket.　　T　(F)
3 Only children are allowed to take water guns on the plane.　　T　(F)
4 The man didn't want to put his bag through the X-ray machine.　　(T)　F
5 A woman did not want a window seat because she was worried the wind would ruin her hair.　　(T)　F

Download *Sounds Good* Podcast 30

Now listen to Podcast 30. You can do the activities, read the transcript, or simpy enjoy listening to young people from around the world.

45

Go online!

Students can visit the *Sounds Good* website at *www.sounds-good-online.com* and click on *Go online!* for extra listening practice based on the unit topic.

Online listening

This section can be used in two ways.

Students can use this for some optional, self-study listening practice outside the classroom. Students will see the same activity as printed in their Student Book and they will be able to complete it online, with immediate feedback on their answer choices.

Alternatively, you can use this section in class as an extension activity. The Online listening is recorded on the Class CDs for this purpose.

Students will listen to a talk by an airport worker, describing some of the odd things he has seen or heard around the airport.

Audio script [CD2, track 35]

Man I work at the airport so I see a lot of different people, and I see many who are upset. Why are they upset? Well, there are quite a few reasons. One reason is that people forget things. They forget their passports or, if they have their passports, they forget to get their visas. If you're going to some countries and don't have your visa, you just can't get on the plane. Forgetting your ticket is not such a big deal anymore as long as you have some identification. They can look up your ticket or you can use a credit card and get another one.

I always have a good laugh at the things you can find at the airport lost property office. Some people get panicked when they hear their flight is boarding and rush to the boarding gate leaving behind all kinds of stuff—bags of shopping, computers, guitars … and snowboards.

Then people have to go to the X-ray machine and it's quite surprising what people try to take on the plane. Of course, there are lots of things you're not allowed to take—even a kid's toy water gun isn't allowed. But people try to carry surprising things in their bags onto flights. Uh … for example, one man didn't want to put his bag through the X-ray machine. Why? What was the problem?

Then we heard it. Woof, woof! He had a small dog in the bag.

Well, my favorite story is about a woman who wouldn't sit in the window seat. Why not? She'd just been to the hair salon before the flight. She was afraid the wind would ruin her hair. Let me tell you something: if you open a window at ten thousand meters, your hair is the last thing you worry about.

Podcast 30

Encourage students to download Podcast 30. Inspired by the unit topic, it is authentic and high-interest, and features young people from around the world.

Sounds delicious!

Goals
- Identifying different types of food
- Understanding different table manners

Learn the language

A 🔵3 🔵2 **What is your favorite food? Match the words A–G to the pictures. Then listen and write down how you eat them. Use the words from the box.**

A tacos   **B** steak   **C** pizza   **D** soup

E dumplings   **F** tempura   **G** Korean barbecued ribs

> hands   knife and fork
> spoon   chopsticks

G
chopsticks

A
hands

B
knife and fork

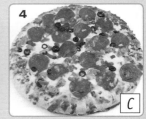
C
hands

D
spoon

E
chopsticks

F
chopsticks

FOCUS

B 🔵3 🔵3 **Listen and match the sentences.**

1 In Western restaurants, it's common to order your own food.   _D_
2 In Chinese restaurants, dinner features lots of different dishes.   _C_
3 At a potluck dinner, no one arrives empty-handed.   _A_
4 When I was a kid, I was always told not to slurp my soup.   _B_

A Everyone brings a dish to share.
B I could never sip it quietly from the side of the spoon.
C People usually share them.
D The main course is usually served on one big plate.

48

Unit overview

The topic of this unit is international food and cultural differences for table manners. In Listening task one, students will listen to four people talking about their food experiences. In Listening task two, students will listen to Julia Primavera, a famous chef, talking about her life. In the speaking activities, students will have an opportunity to use description skills to talk about a local food.

Learn the language

- Ask students about their favorite foods. Which ones do they like to eat at home and which ones do they like to eat in restaurants? How do they eat each food: with their hands, a knife and fork, a spoon or chopsticks?

- Have students open the book and look at the pictures. Ask them what food is shown in each picture.

- Read the words (A–G) and ask students to match them to the pictures.

- Allow students a few minutes to finish writing the answers.

- Explain that students will listen to the audio and write down the way to eat each food. Tell students that in different places, foods are eaten in different ways. For example, many people eat pizza using their hands while others eat pizza using a knife and fork.

- Have students go over the words in the box quickly.

- Play the audio (CD3, track 2) and have students write down the words under the pictures.

- Review the answers with students by playing the audio again. Stop the CD and play each sentence again as often as necessary.

Audio script [CD3, track 2]

1 Korean barbecued ribs. You can use chopsticks to eat Korean barbecued ribs.
2 Tacos. You can eat tacos with your hands.
3 Steak. You use a knife and fork to eat steak.
4 Pizza. You can eat pizza with your hands.
5 Soup. You usually use a spoon to eat soup.
6 Dumplings. You use chopsticks to pick up the dumplings.
7 Tempura. You use chopsticks to eat tempura.

B

- Have students read through the sentences to get an idea of what they will be listening for.

- Play the audio (CD3, track 3) and have students match the sentences.

- Review the language to make sure students understand everything.

Language note

A *dish* can refer to a serving plate or the food that is served on it.

Audio script [CD3, track 3]

1
Woman In Western restaurants, it's common to order your own food. The main course is usually served on one big plate.

2
Man In Chinese restaurants, dinner features lots of different dishes. People usually share them.

3
Woman At a potluck dinner, no one arrives empty-handed. Everyone brings a dish to share.

4
Man When I was a kid, I was always told not to slurp my soup. I could never sip it quietly from the side of the spoon.

Listening task one

A **3** [4-7] Listen for attitudes Four people are talking about different food experiences. What are the things that surprise them? Listen and check ☑ the correct pictures.

1

2

3

4

B **3** [4-7] Listen for comparison and contrast Why are the speakers surprised? Listen again and number the correct answers.

speaker

A He isn't used to people bringing dishes to share. _2_

B In her country, people use a spoon to eat soup. _4_

C She is used to people sharing dishes in Chinese restaurants. _1_

D In his country, different foods are usually served together on the same plate. _3_

Speak out!

Work with a partner. Look at the pictures above. Do any of the things surprise you? Tell your partner.

Use the language in **FOCUS** to help you.

49

Listening task one

A

- Tell students that they will listen to four people talking about their food experiences. They need to find out the things that surprised them.

- Have students look at the pictures and say what is shown in each picture.

- Play the audio (CD3, tracks 4–7) and have students check the correct pictures. Point out that the first speaker is Taiwanese, the second speaker is Korean, the third is Australian and the fourth is British.

- Review the answers with students. Ask students what words and phrases helped them decide the correct picture for each talk.

Audio script [CD3, tracks 4–7]

1

Woman In Taipei, where I come from, there are many American restaurants so I know it's common to order your own food instead of sharing several dishes. I'm used to the idea. But when I moved to Chicago, one thing really surprised me. We went out to a Chinese restaurant and the people I went with still ordered separate dishes.

2

Man When I first moved to California, I was invited to a potluck dinner. I knew I was invited to a dinner, but I didn't understand what 'potluck' meant—and didn't ask! Of course, I arrived empty-handed, and I was surprised that everyone had brought a dish to share. I felt so embarrassed! But everyone understood and we had a good laugh about it.

3

Man When I was growing up in Australia, dinner always featured the same foods: meat and vegetables all served together on one big plate. When I traveled to China, I was surprised to find that dinner featured lots of little dishes and my plate was really small. I could pick small pieces of food out of the dishes I liked—stir-fries, shrimp dumplings, steamed fish and vegetables.

4

Woman As a kid growing up in England, I loved soup, but I could never sip it quietly from the side of the spoon. I was always told not to slurp or put the whole spoon in my mouth. So when I visited Japan, I really enjoyed my miso soup. I could drink it right from the bowl.

B

- Tell students that they are going to listen again to find out why the speakers are surprised. Tell them that they need to match the reasons to the correct speakers.

- Have students read through the statements.

- Play the audio (CD3, tracks 4–7) again and have students number the statements.

- Review the answers with students. If necessary, play the audio again.

Speak out!

- Review the language in the *Focus* box on the previous Student Book page.

- Put students into pairs and explain the speaking activity.

Model conversation

A This woman was told not to slurp her soup when she was a kid, but it's OK to slurp your soup in this country.

B Yes, that's surprising.

Extension

Have pairs talk about other surprising food experiences they have heard about or experienced. Encourage students to talk about appropriate table manners for an unfamiliar meal. For example, it is usually best to observe what others around you are doing first and then do the same thing.

Unit 7

Listening task two

A **3** **8** Listen for key details Julia Primavera is being interviewed about her life as a chef. What is her most popular signature dish? Listen and check ☑ the correct picture.

1

☐

3

☐

2

☐

4

☐

B **3** **8** Listen for specific information Listen again and choose the correct answers.

1   What types of food did Julia first learn to cook?
   A   Italian and American.
   B   Mexican and American.
   C   Italian and Mexican.

2   What made Julia want to be a chef?
   A   Working at her parent's restaurant.
   B   A trip to Asia where she tried new foods.
   C   A chance to go backpacking in Mexico.

3   Why is her grandmother's cookbook her favorite?
   A   It has 200 Italian recipes.
   B   It taught her to be passionate about cooking.
   C   It has a great recipe for stir-fries.

4   Why are Julia's dishes so popular?
   A   She uses expensive ingredients.
   B   She uses quality ingredients.
   C   They are from her grandmother's cookbook.

5   What are the main ingredients in Julia's Stir Fry?
   A   Shrimp, tomatoes, chilies and herbs.
   B   Clams, tomatoes, chilies and herbs.
   C   Clams, shrimp, vegetables and herbs.

Speak out!   **3** **8** Work with a partner. Listen again and take notes of the questions that the interviewer asks Julia. Think about some other questions that you want to ask Julia. Discuss them with your partner.

50

Listening task two

- The new language introduced in this section includes the following words, phrases and sentences:

  celebrity chef
  Mexican food
  cookbook
  be passionate about cooking
  What makes a signature dish?
  It's important to start with the right ingredients.
  recipe
  clams stir-fried with tomatoes, chilies and herbs

- Ask students if they know the names of any famous chefs doing cooking shows on TV. Who are they? What kinds of food do they cook?

- Have students look at the pictures and say what food is shown in each picture.

- Explain that students will listen to an interview with Julia Primavera, a famous chef. Students need to find out what her most popular signature dish—the dish that Julia is famous for—is.

- Play the audio (CD3, track 8) and have students check the correct picture.

- Ask students what ingredients are in Julia's most popular dish.

Audio script [CD3, track 8]

Man Welcome to *Twenty Questions*. Today, we're talking to celebrity chef Julia Primavera. Julia, let's start with the first question. Did you cook growing up?

Julia Oh, yeah. As a kid, I started working in my parents' restaurant. We had a small seafood place—Italian, of course—in San Diego. I did small jobs like peeling shrimp or chopping up vegetables. It wasn't long before they let me near the stove. When you're a kid, you learn quickly.

Man So it was Italian food that you first learned to cook?

Julia Yeah, that and Mexican food. San Diego is just a short drive from Mexico, so people eat a lot of tacos.

Man Did you always want to be a chef?

Julia Oh, no! I couldn't wait to get out of the kitchen. When I finished school, I traveled through Asia for a few months, you know, backpacking. I fell in love with food all over again … Korean barbecued ribs, Japanese tempura, Chinese stir-fries and dumplings. There were so many new tastes and ingredients for me. When I came

back, I knew I wanted to spend the rest of my life cooking.

Man Do you have a favorite cookbook?

Julia I have over two hundred cookbooks, but my favorite is an old one—my grandmother's *Italian Home Cooking*. The book taught me not to worry about rules and be passionate about cooking.

Man We know that you worked in many restaurants throughout the US and created a few excellent dishes. What makes a signature dish?

Julia Well, I never thought about creating signature dishes, but it just happened. It's important to start with the right ingredients and think about the people you're cooking for.

Man Your most popular signature dish is Julia's Stir Fry. What's the secret behind it?

Julia The quality ingredients! It's a simple recipe— clams stir-fried with tomatoes, chilies and herbs.

Man Sounds delicious.

- Have students read through the questions on the page to get an idea of what specific information they need to listen for.

- Play the audio (CD3, track 8) again and have students choose the correct answers.

- Review the answers with students.

Speak out!

- The aim of this section is to integrate listening with other skills. In this case, students practice note-taking, writing questions and speaking.

- Put students into pairs and explain the speaking activity.

- Play the audio (CD3, track 8) once more and have students take notes of the questions that the interviewer asks Julia.

- Have students think about some other questions they want to ask Julia and then discuss the questions with their partners.

- Encourage pairs to do the discussion as if they were Julia and the interviewer.

Model conversation

A How many hours a day do you work?

B Quite a few. I go to the market at around six o'clock in the morning to find fresh fish and vegetables. And I don't leave the restaurant until midnight.

A How about Sundays?

B Sundays I don't have to work at all. I spend the time with my family.

Write what you hear

A (3 9) The sounds /t/ and /d/ at the end of words may be difficult to hear because they are sometimes silent or blend together with the sound that follows. The past tense ending *-ed*, however, is never silent. Listen and complete the sentences.

Example: (I wanted to spend the rest of my life cooking.) → I ____*wanted to spend the rest of*____ my life cooking.

1 I ____*started working*____ in my parents' restaurant.

2 We had a small ____*seafood place*____ .

3 Do you have a ____*favorite cookbook*____ ?

4 So it was Italian ____*food that*____ you ____*first learned to*____ cook?

5 San Diego ____*is just a short drive*____ from Mexico.

6 I couldn't ____*wait to get out of*____ the kitchen.

7 The book ____*taught me not to*____ worry ____*about rules*____ and be ____*passionate about*____ cooking.

8 It's ____*important to start with the*____ right ingredients ____*and think about the*____ people you're cooking for.

B (3 9) Now listen again and repeat. Try saying the sentences as naturally as possible.

Use what you learn

A Think about a food that visitors to your country would find interesting. Complete the table below. (Answers may vary.)

Name of the food	sushi
Ingredients	– raw fish – rice – vinegar – wasabi
How do you eat it?	– with chopsticks – with hands

B Work with a partner. Read the description of the ingredients and how you eat the food and let your partner guess what it is. Take turns.

A You use rice and raw fish to make it. You can eat it with chopsticks or with your hands.

B Is it sushi?

A That's right.

51

Write what you hear

Aim

The aim of this section is for students to identify and correctly pronounce the sounds /t/ and /d/ at the end of words including past tense forms ending in *-ed*.

The letters 't' and 'd' are pronounced as /t/ and /d/ respectively: /t/ is a voiceless sound, while /d/ is a voiced sound. When the sounds /t/ and /d/ appear at the end of words in sentences they may be difficult to hear. They may be either silent or blend together with the sound that follows.

However, the past tense ending, *-ed*, is never silent. Its pronunciation depends on the verb to which it is attached. When the verb ends with a voiceless consonant like /p/, /k/, /f/, /ʃ/, /tʃ/, /s/ or /θ/, the ending *-ed* is pronounced as /t/, e.g., *finished* /ˈfɪnɪʃt/. When the verb ends with a voiced consonant like /b/, /g/, /v/, /ʒ/, /dʒ/, /z/, /ð/ or sounds like /l/, /m/ and /n/ or a vowel, *-ed* is pronounced as /d/, e.g., *learned* /ˈlɜrnd/. When the verb ends with the sounds /t/ or /d/, *-ed* is pronounced as /ɪd/, e.g., *started* /ˈstɑrtɪd/.

- Introduce the sounds /t/ and /d/ at the end of words and the pronunciation of /t/ and /d/ in the past tense ending *-ed*.

- Point out the example and model the sentence.

- Play the audio (CD3, track 9) and have students fill in the missing words.

- Have some students write their answers on the board. Play the audio again to review the answers. Encourage students to find and correct any of their mistakes.

Audio script [CD3, track 9]

Example: I wanted to spend the rest of my life cooking.
1 I started working in my parents' restaurant.
2 We had a small seafood place.
3 Do you have a favorite cookbook?
4 So it was Italian food that you first learned to cook?
5 San Diego is just a short drive from Mexico.
6 I couldn't wait to get out of the kitchen.
7 The book taught me not to worry about rules and be passionate about cooking.
8 It's important to start with the right ingredients and think about the people you're cooking for.

- Play the audio (CD3, track 9) again. Have students repeat each sentence out loud, paying special attention to the pronunciation of the /t/ and /d/ sounds.

- Monitor and provide feedback on students' pronunciation.

Use what you learn

Aim

The aim of this section is to give students the opportunity to use description skills to talk about a local food.

- Review the unit vocabulary and functional language by talking about your favorite foods and asking students about their favorite foods.

- Have students work individually to complete the table about an interesting local food.

- Explain the activity and model the sentences at the bottom of the page with a student.

- Put students into pairs and have them describe and guess the food in turns. Encourage students to think of unusual dishes that other students may not be familiar with.

Extension

Ask students to survey each other and make a list of popular local dishes that tourists or visitors to their country might find strange to eat.

Unit **7**

Your score:

_____ /10

Test yourself

3 **10** You will hear a question or statement followed by three responses. They are not printed in your book. Choose the best response to each question or statement. Here is an example:

You will hear:

Man How do people usually eat dumplings?

You will also hear:

Woman **A** Yes, they do.
B Dumplings are very popular in China.
C They usually eat them with chopsticks.

The best response to the question "How do people usually eat dumplings?" is choice C, "They usually eat them with chopsticks.", so you should circle C.

3 **11** Now listen to ten questions and statements, each followed by three responses. Choose the best response to each question or statement.

1 A (B) C		6 A B (C)
2 A B (C)		7 (A) B C
3 A (B) C		8 A (B) C
4 A B (C)		9 A B (C)
5 (A) B C		10 (A) B C

52

Test yourself

Aim

The aim of this section is to provide exam practice. Students will listen to some questions and statements and choose the best response to each question or statement from three response choices.

Explain the test format. Students will have seven seconds after each question to choose the best response. Neither the questions and statements nor the response choices are printed in the book, so students should focus on the question or statement and predict a possible response.

Play the example (CD3, track 10). Explain that the question requires a response about the way people eat dumplings. The only appropriate response should be the one about the way people eat dumplings.

Audio script [CD3, track 10]

Man   How do people usually eat dumplings?
A   Yes, they do.
B   Dumplings are very popular in China.
C   They usually eat them with chopsticks.

[CD3, track 11]

1   What's your favorite dish?
 A   I use a knife and fork.
 B   I really like barbecued ribs.
 C   I don't like tacos.

2   So it was French food that you first learned to cook?
 A   Yes, I like French food very much.
 B   Yes, French food is very expensive.
 C   Yes, I learned to cook French food when I was growing up.

3   We're invited to a potluck dinner on Saturday.
 A   I hope the food is not expensive.
 B   OK, we can bring some tacos and sushi.
 C   I hope it's a good restaurant.

4   Do we share several dishes or do we order our own food?
 A   This stir-fry is delicious.
 B   No, I don't like sushi.
 C   It's a Chinese restaurant, so we can share.

5   What's your signature dish?
 A   It's pasta with clams and fresh tomatoes.
 B   It's a simple recipe from a Japanese cookbook.
 C   I like to cook with fresh ingredients.

6   Did you always want to be a chef?
 A   Yes, I always use a cookbook.
 B   No, I never liked cooking for other people.
 C   Yes, I always liked creating dishes.

7   Did you arrive at the dinner empty-handed?
 A   Yes, I didn't know it was a potluck dinner.
 B   Yes, I brought lots of presents.
 C   No, I arrived on time.

8   Is it common to share dishes here?
 A   Yes, but it's easier to use your hands.
 B   No, usually everyone orders their own dish.
 C   No, use a spoon.

9   Do I use a spoon to eat miso soup?
 A   No, it's common to eat it with a knife and fork.
 B   Yes, miso soup tastes good.
 C   No, you can drink it right from the bowl.

10   I was surprised that all my food was served on one big plate.
 A   Well, it is common to serve the meat, rice and vegetables together.
 B   Well, it is common to share several dishes.
 C   Well, you can use your hands to eat.

Go online!

Visit the *Sounds Good* website at **www.sounds-good-online.com**
Click on **Go online!** for extra listening practice.

Online listening

A **3** **12** Listen for key words Jane is talking about the meal she is making for her friend Min-Yi. Listen and check ☑ the ingredients that she is using.

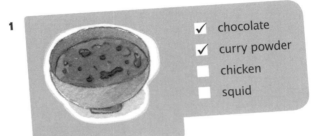

1
- ☑ chocolate
- ☑ curry powder
- ☐ chicken
- ☐ squid

2
- ☑ squid
- ☐ clams
- ☐ vegetables
- ☑ cheese

3
- ☑ watermelon
- ☐ raw fish
- ☐ tomatoes
- ☐ eggs

B **3** **12** Listen for specific information Listen again and circle the correct answers.

1 What meal are Jane and Min-Yi having?
- **A** Breakfast.
- **B** Lunch.
- **(C)** Dinner.

2 Did Jane use a cookbook for the first dish?
- **(A)** No, she made it up herself.
- **B** Yes, but she changed it a bit.
- **C** No, she got the recipe from her mom.

3 What is Jane not sure about?
- **A** The appetizers.
- **B** The main course.
- **(C)** The dessert.

4 What does Jane want to make for dessert?
- **A** Sushi or salad.
- **(B)** Sushi or tacos.
- **C** Tacos or dumplings.

Download *Sounds Good* Podcast 31

Now listen to Podcast 31. You can do the activities, read the transcript, or simpy enjoy listening to young people from around the world.

Go online!

Students can visit the *Sounds Good* website at *www.sounds-good-online.com* and click on *Go online!* for extra listening practice based on the unit topic.

Online listening

This section can be used in two ways.

Students can use this for some optional, self-study listening practice outside the classroom. Students will see the same activity as printed in their Student Book and they will be able to complete it online, with immediate feedback on their answer choices.

Alternatively, you can use this section in class as an extension activity. The Online listening is recorded on the Class CDs for this purpose.

Students will listen to a conversation between Min-Yi and his friend Jane. Jane is making a special dinner for Min-Yi. Jane has an Australian accent.

Audio script [CD3, track 12]

Min-Yi Well, Jane, thanks so much for inviting me for dinner.

Jane Oh, no, Min-Yi. It's really nice of you to come. I mean, I really like cooking for other people.

Min-Yi Really? How did you learn cooking? I mean, did anyone teach you?

Jane No. I just learned … it's easy. I just think about the person I'm cooking for and create a dish.

Min-Yi So, what are you making?

Jane I wanted to try something really different … can you smell it?

Min-Yi I, uh … it smells like … curry. Curry and … chocolate.

Jane Exactly! That's it. I've made a chocolate curry! I hope you like chocolate and curry.

Min-Yi Yes, but not usually at the same time. Um, you didn't use a cookbook?

Jane Oh, no. I made it up myself. I hope you like it!

Min-Yi I'm sure it will be … different. What else are you making?

Jane Well, I'm also making squid dumplings with lots of cheese.

Min-Yi Let me guess, this is not from a cookbook either?

Jane Right again! But I'm still not sure what I should make for dessert.

Min-Yi Oh, we could always go out for dessert.

Jane Don't be silly. I really love to cook and there are a couple of dishes I could make. They both have watermelon in them.

Min-Yi Oh, good! I love watermelon. We can just have watermelon for dessert.

Jane Oh, no—I want to make you something special!

Min-Yi But you really don't have to—

Jane So, what do you prefer, Japanese or Mexican?

Min-Yi Japanese or Mexican? Uh … why do you ask?

Jane I want to make watermelon sushi or watermelon tacos.

Podcast 31

Encourage students to download Podcast 31. Inspired by the unit topic, it is authentic and high-interest, and features young people from around the world.

8 I'm thinking of getting fit.

Goals
- Understanding fitness and diet options
- Identifying personal workouts and diets

Learn the language

A 3 13 **How do you keep fit and stay healthy? Read the sentences and match them to the pictures. Then listen and number the pictures.**

A Lift some weights. **B** Go for a run. **C** Never take elevators or escalators.

D Go for a long walk. **E** Do some yoga. **F** Do some sit-ups. **G** Do some push-ups.

H Walk up and down the stairs.

 H 4
 A 5
 F 1
 B 7

 C 2
 E 6
 D 3
 G 8

FOCUS

B 3 14 **Listen and fill in the blanks with the words from the box.**

shape   portions   exercise   car   watch   healthy food   fitness club

1   How do I keep in great ___*shape*___? Well, I joined a ___*fitness club*___ and work out a lot.

2   I eat a lot of ___*healthy food*___.

3   I ___*watch*___ what I eat, and I eat small ___*portions*___ of food.

4   I turn everything into ___*exercise*___.

5   I never use my ___*car*___ if I don't have to.

54

96

Unit overview

The topic of this unit is health and fitness. In Listening task one, students will listen to Helen and Emily talking about diet and fitness practices. In Listening task two, students will listen to six people talking about their lifestyles, including their diet and the things they do to keep fit. In the speaking activities, students will have an opportunity to talk about their diet and the exercise they do to keep fit.

Learn the language

- Ask students what they do to keep fit—through exercise and/or diet. Ask them what sorts of fitness routines they have or would consider adopting in order to get fit.

- Have students open the book and look at the pictures. Ask them what the people are doing in each picture.

- Read the sentences (A–H) and ask students to match them to the pictures.

- Allow students a few minutes to finish writing the answers.

- Play the audio (CD3, track 13) and have students number the pictures.

- Review the answers with students by playing the audio again. Stop the CD and play each sentence again as often as necessary.

Audio script [CD3, track 13]

1. Do some sit-ups.
2. Never take elevators or escalators.
3. Go for a long walk.
4. Walk up and down the stairs.
5. Lift some weights.
6. Do some yoga.
7. Go for a run.
8. Do some push-ups.

B

- Have students read through the words and the sentences to get an idea of what they will be listening for.

- Play the audio (CD3, track 14) and have students fill in the blanks.

- Review the answers with students by playing the audio again.

- Have students role-play saying the sentences in the *Focus* box as if they were telling something about themselves.

Language note

To *work out* is to make your body fit and strong by doing exercise.

Another common word for a *fitness club* is a *gym*. They have exactly the same meaning.

Audio script [CD3, track 14]

1. How do I keep in great shape? Well, I joined a fitness club and work out a lot.
2. I eat a lot of healthy food.
3. I watch what I eat, and I eat small portions of food.
4. I turn everything into exercise.
5. I never use my car if I don't have to.

Listening task one

A **3** **15** Listen for main ideas Helen and Emily are talking. Listen and choose the correct answers.

1 Do Helen and Emily already know each other?

(A) Yes.
B No.

2 Why is Emily asking Helen questions?

A Emily wants Helen to get fit.
(B) Emily wants to get fit.

3 What does Helen think is most important?

(A) Start by doing something.
B Get fit first.

B **3** **16** Listen for sequence Helen has a lot of ideas and advice about exercise and health. Listen and number the ideas in the order Helen mentions them.

A

4

B

3

C

1

D

5

E

2

F

6

C **3** **16** Listen for feelings What does Emily like and dislike? Listen again and choose the correct answers.

1 Emily (likes)/ doesn't like to drink cappuccino.
2 Emily likes /(doesn't like) to drink green tea.
3 Emily likes /(doesn't like) running in the rain.
4 Emily (likes)/ doesn't like using her car.
5 Emily likes /(doesn't like) eating small portions.
6 Emily likes /(doesn't like) to go for walks after dinner.

Speak out!

Work with a partner. Do you do any of the same things that Helen does? Tell your partner.

Use the language in **FOCUS** to help you.

55

Listening task one

- Introduce the two characters, Helen and Emily. Emily has a Canadian accent. Explain that students will listen to a conversation between them about keeping fit.

- Have students read through the questions to get an idea of what they will be listening for.

- Play the audio (CD3, track 15) and have students choose the correct answers.

- Review the answers with students.

- Ask students which words or phrases helped them decide the correct answer for each question, e.g., *Emily calls out Helen's name directly, so they must know each other already.*

Audio script [CD3, track 15]

Emily You look good, Helen. How do you keep in such great shape?

Helen Well, I work out a lot.

Emily Really, I'm thinking of getting fit.

Helen You can't just think about it. You have to do something about it.

Emily Yeah, I know. But where do I start?

Helen You can join a fitness club. I joined one last year and go a few times a week.

Emily Is that all you do?

Helen No. But it's a good start.

- Put students into pairs and have them discuss what is shown in each of the pictures.

- Explain that Helen is giving Emily ideas and advice on how to get fit and stay healthy.

- Play the audio (CD3, track 16) and have students number the ideas and advice in the order Helen mentions them.

- Review the answers with students.

Audio script [CD3, track 16]

Emily OK, Helen. Let's talk about what I should do to get fit. Do you want to grab a cappuccino? There's a café right here.

Helen Oh, no, Emily! Cut out the cappuccinos and the little snacks. Let's have some green tea.

Emily Uh … I don't really like green tea. Anyway, we can sit over there and—

Helen Sit? Why sit when you can walk? Why walk when you can run? Why run when you can run faster?

Emily Uh, I don't think I can run with a cup of tea when it's raining.

Helen OK. But let's walk. It's hardly raining at all.

Emily So, you exercise twenty-four seven?

Helen Pretty much. I never take elevators or escalators any more. I always walk up and down the stairs. I got a bicycle and never use my car if I don't have to.

Emily Wow. I couldn't live without my car. And do you eat anything special?

Helen I mostly eat natural, healthy foods and I don't eat dessert. Most importantly, I watch what I eat.

Emily You watch what you eat?

Helen Yep, I eat lots of fruits and vegetables, and don't eat snacks between meals. Also, I eat small portions—you know, small amounts. Use small plates to make your food look bigger.

Emily But I'd get too hungry!

Helen No, drink lots of water and you feel less hungry. And of course, don't forget to exercise!

Emily So … how often do you exercise?

Helen On an average day? I go to my fitness club most mornings, and do yoga before breakfast. I often lift weights during my lunch break, and after dinner I go for a long walk. Why don't you come for a walk with me tonight?

Emily But I'm so tired after dinner. And I'll miss my favorite TV shows!

- Have students read through the sentences.

- Play the audio (CD3, track 16) again and have students circle the correct words.

- Put students into pairs and have them compare their answers. How would they describe Helen's personality and Emily's personality?

Speak out!

- Review the language in the *Focus* box on the previous Student Book page.

- Put students into pairs and explain the speaking activity.

- Have some students tell the class what they do to keep fit.

Model conversation

A Do you do any of the things Helen does?

B A couple, but not all of them. I drink green tea.

A Do you go for a walk after dinner?

B Yes. I usually go for a long walk with my sister.

Unit 8

Listening task two

A **3** **17-22** Listen for main ideas Six speakers are talking about their lifestyles. Read the summaries below. Then listen and number them.

__2__ Stay healthy by doing activities you love and eating healthy food.

__1__ Keep fit by walking at least thirty minutes every day.

__5__ Play lots of sports if you eat unhealthy food.

__3__ Make your trip to work and other places a part of your exercise routine.

__6__ Watch what you eat if you do not like to exercise.

__4__ Exercise on your own to keep fit.

B **3** **17-22** Listen for key words Listen again and write the things that the six people do. Use the phrases in the box to help you.

> cycling   dancing   doing push-ups   doing sit-ups   eating healthy food   eating junk food
> hanging out   not eating too many snacks   playing lots of sports   rollerblading   walking
> watching movies and reading

1  *hanging out* *walking*

4  *doing push-ups* *doing sit-ups*

2  *eating healthy food* *dancing*

5  *eating junk food* *playing lots of sports*

3  *cycling* *rollerblading*

6  *watching movies and reading* *not eating too many snacks*

Speak out! **3** **17-22** Work with a partner. Listen again and make a list of the different ways people mention to keep fit and stay healthy. Discuss your answers with your partner and decide on the three best ways.

56

Listening task two

- The new language introduced in this section includes the following phrases and sentences:

    What do I do to keep fit?
    a bit skinny
    I'd rather hang out with my friends than sweat in a gym.
    go rollerblading
    A lot of people find an excuse not to exercise,
    junk food
    I always felt uncomfortable playing games or running.

- Explain that students will listen to six people talking about their lifestyles. Students need to number the summaries for the talks in the order they hear them.

- Have students read through the summaries on the page.

- Play the audio (CD3, tracks 17–22) and have students number the summaries. Point out that the first speaker has an Australian accent, the third speaker has a Korean accent and the sixth speaker has a Canadian accent.

Audio script [CD3, tracks 17–22]

1
Man   What do I do to keep fit? Actually, I don't do anything. I've always been a bit skinny and have never found an activity that suits me. I'd rather hang out with my friends than sweat in a gym. But I make sure that I walk at least thirty minutes every day.

2
Woman   How do I stay healthy? Two things, really. I keep lots of healthy food in my fridge … salad stuff, fresh fruit and vegetables, that sort of thing. I also dance. I love dancing, so I go to clubs with my friends and dance all night.

3
Man   I hate working out. I think it's boring. But I don't have a car. I stopped driving years ago and bought a good bicycle. Now I get all my exercise going places—to work, shopping, to go see my friends. Sometimes, instead of cycling, I go rollerblading.

4
Man   A lot of people find an excuse not to exercise, "It's cold so I can't run. It's late so my club's closed. My partner's busy so I can't play tennis." But not me. I do two things to keep in shape: push-ups and sit-ups. I can do them anywhere.

5
Woman   OK, I admit it. I do eat a lot of junk food, I'm afraid, but I also play a lot of sports. I have a different sport for each season … skiing in winter, soccer in spring, baseball in the summer and badminton in autumn.

6
Woman   Exercise is a waste of time! There are so many other things that I enjoy doing, such as watching a movie or reading a good book. I never liked doing sports at school either. I always felt uncomfortable playing games or running. I wouldn't even run to catch the bus! But I watch what I eat, and I don't eat too many snacks.

B

- Ask students to read through the phrases for different activities in the box.

- Play the audio (CD3, tracks 17–22) again and have students write the things the six people do in the speech bubbles.

- Review the answers with students by asking students what each person does.

Speak out!

- The aim of this section is to integrate listening with other skills. In this case, students practice note-taking before giving their opinions in a discussion.

- Put students into pairs and explain the speaking activity.

- Play the audio (CD3, tracks 17–22) once more and have students make a list of the ways people mention to keep fit and stay healthy.

- Have students discuss their answers with their partners and decide on the three best ways.

- Encourage students to give reasons for their choices of the three best ways.

Model conversation

A   The best way to keep fit is to eat healthy food.
B   I agree. It's really important and everyone can do it.

101

Learn the rhythm

 A **3** **23** Some words in a sentence are stressed and sound strong while others are not stressed and sound weak. Listen and underline the strong words.

Example: I'm <u>thinking</u> of <u>getting</u> <u>fit</u>.

1 And after <u>dinner</u> I <u>go</u> for a <u>long</u> <u>walk</u>.

2 We can <u>sit</u> over <u>there</u>.

3 Let's <u>have</u> some <u>green</u> <u>tea</u>.

4 <u>Why</u> <u>don't</u> you <u>come</u> for a <u>walk</u> with me <u>tonight</u>?

5 I <u>always</u> <u>walk</u> <u>up</u> and <u>down</u> the <u>stairs</u>.

6 I'll <u>miss</u> my <u>favorite</u> <u>TV</u> <u>shows</u>.

7 I <u>eat</u> <u>lots</u> of <u>fruit</u> and <u>vegetables</u>, and don't <u>eat</u> <u>snacks</u> between <u>meals</u>.

8 I <u>go</u> to my <u>fitness</u> <u>club</u> <u>most</u> <u>mornings</u> and <u>do</u> <u>yoga</u> before <u>breakfast</u>.

B **3** **23** Now listen again and repeat. Try saying the weak words faster and quieter than the strong words.

Use what you learn

A How healthy are you? Add two more healthy things to the table then check ☑ how often you do each thing. *Answers may vary.*

How often do you …	never	once a week	more than once a week	every day
do yoga?			✓	
go for a run?		✓		
eat fruit and vegetables?				✓
eat healthy meals?			✓	
go for a walk?		✓		

Now add up your score:

never	0pts	more than once a week	2pts
once a week	1pt	every day	3pts

Your score: ___9___

12–15 points: You are an Olympic athlete!

8–11 points: Could you be my fitness coach?

3–7 points: Maybe you need to spend less time on the couch!

0–2 points: Check your heart! Are you still alive?

B Work in groups of three. Interview each other about how often you exercise and what you eat and drink. Take turns.

A How often do you do yoga?

B Three times a week.

C Do you go to a fitness club?

B No, I don't.

57

Learn the rhythm

Aim

The aim of this section is for students to distinguish between strong and weak words in connected speech and to practice rhythms of strong and weak words.

A sentence has strong and weak words. Strong words are usually content words and are stressed. Content words include *nouns, adjectives, verbs, adverbs* and *question words*.

Weak words are often function words and are not usually stressed. Function words include *personal* and *possessive pronouns, prepositions, conjunctions* and *auxiliary verbs*. The alternating pattern of strong and weak words in a sentence makes a rhythm. The strong syllables in strong words get more time than the unstressed syllables and weak words are spoken quickly.

- Introduce the topic of strong and weak words.
- Point out the example and model the sentence. Point out the strong and weak words in the sentence.
- Play the audio (CD3, track 23) and have students underline the strong words.
- Write the sentences on the board. Play the audio again. Pause the audio after each sentence and ask students for their answers. Encourage students to find and correct any of their mistakes.

Audio script [CD3, track 23]

Example: I'm thinking of getting fit.
1 And after dinner I go for a long walk.
2 We can sit over there.
3 Let's have some green tea.
4 Why don't you come for a walk with me tonight?
5 I always walk up and down the stairs.
6 I'll miss my favorite TV shows.
7 I eat lots of fruit and vegetables, and don't eat snacks between meals.
8 I go to my fitness club most mornings and do yoga before breakfast.

B

- Play the audio (CD3, track 23) again. Have students repeat the sentences out loud, paying special attention to the rhythm of strong words and weak words in the sentences.
- Monitor and provide feedback on students' pronunciation.

Use what you learn

Aim

The aim of this section is to give students the opportunity to talk about their diet and the exercise they do.

A

- Review the unit vocabulary and functional language by asking students about the ways they keep fit and stay healthy.
- Explain that *pts* is short for *points*.
- Have students work individually to complete the table.

B

- Explain the activity and model the sentences at the bottom of the page with three students.
- Put students into groups of three and have them work together to complete the activity.
- Ask some students to tell the class how often they exercise and what they usually eat and drink.

Unit **8**

Test yourself

3 **24** **You will hear three conversations. You will be asked to answer three questions about each conversation. Choose the best response to each question.**

1 What does Satoshi do at the fitness club?

A Lifting weights and doing some exercise.
B Running and lifting weights.
C Lifting weights and some yoga.
D Swimming and skiing.

2 How often does Satoshi go to the fitness club?

A Once a week.
B Twice a week.
C Three times a week.
D Three or four times a week.

3 What else does Satoshi do to keep fit?

A Plays a few sports.
B Swimming.
C Skiing.
D Swimming and running.

4 Why is Danny NOT sure about going to lunch?

A He is afraid that the food won't be healthy.
B He doesn't like barbecued ribs.
C He had barbecued ribs for lunch yesterday.
D He has already had lunch.

5 Why does Danny decide to go to lunch?

A The barbecued ribs are really good.
B The restaurant serves tacos too.
C He hasn't eaten barbecued ribs in a really long time.
D The restaurant also serves healthy food.

6 Why is Danny serious about fitness?

A He gets sick a lot.
B He wants to keep in shape so he is healthy in his old age.
C He does not go to a fitness club.
D He likes doing push-ups.

7 What does Ken want?

A He wants Denise to start doing workouts.
B He wants to be in better shape.
C He wants Denise to be in better shape.
D He wants to eat healthy food.

8 What did Ken use to do a few years ago?

A He played a few sports.
B He ate junk food.
C He worked in a fast food restaurant.
D He did workouts.

9 What does Denise suggest?

A She suggests he finish eating all his junk food.
B She suggests he throw out all his junk food.
C She suggests he join a fitness club.
D She suggests he start playing a few sports.

8

58

104

Test yourself

Aim

The aim of this section is to provide exam practice. Students will listen to three short conversations, each followed by three questions, and choose the correct answer from four answer choices.

Explain the test format. Students will have seven seconds after each question to choose the correct answer. Students should read the questions first to get an idea of what specific information they need to listen for.

Audio script [CD3, track 24]

Questions 1 through 3 refer to the following conversation.

Woman Satoshi, you look very fit. What do you do for a workout?
Satoshi Oh, I joined a fitness club a few years ago.
Woman So, what do you do there?
Satoshi The usual, I lift weights and I go running.
Woman How often do you go there?
Satoshi About three times a week, sometimes four. But I usually go for about two hours each time. A lot of people go to a fitness club and just stay for a half-hour yoga class. They don't do a real workout.
Woman How 'bout outside of the fitness club? Do you do anything else?
Satoshi Well, I think once you get fit, you want to do a bit more. I do a few sports, you know, different ones in different seasons.
Woman You mean like swimming in the summer?
Satoshi Yeah, and I do some skiing in the winter.
Woman Good for you.

1 What does Satoshi do at the fitness club?
2 How often does Satoshi go to the fitness club?
3 What else does Satoshi do to keep fit?

Questions 4 through 6 refer to the following conversation.

Danny Hey, Naomi. Where are you going?
Naomi I'm just going to get some lunch, Danny. Do you wanna come?
Danny Uh, sure. Where are you going?
Naomi Oh, there's a fast food place around the corner that has barbecued ribs.
Danny Oh, I don't know. I usually try to eat healthy food.
Naomi Barbequed ribs aren't junk food. Anyway, I'm sure they have some other things there, like salad.
Danny OK, let's go. We can walk down the stairs.

Naomi The stairs?! Don't you want to take the elevator?
Danny No, I always use the stairs.
Naomi But we're on the fourteenth floor!
Danny It doesn't take too long.
Naomi Let me guess, you don't take escalators either.
Danny Not if I can help it.
Naomi Wow, you're quite serious about fitness, aren't you?
Danny Yeah. I do a hundred sit-ups and push-ups everyday. I want to be fit and healthy when I'm old.

4 Why is Danny NOT sure about going to lunch?
5 Why does Danny decide to go to lunch?
6 Why is Danny serious about fitness?

Questions 7 through 9 refer to the following conversation.

Ken Hi, Denise. How are you doing?
Denise Not so bad, Ken. How about you?
Ken Well, I could be better. I'm just not in such great shape anymore.
Denise Anymore? You used to be in good shape?
Ken Well, a while ago—quite a while ago—I used to play a few sports and, you know, do more.
Denise And now?
Ken And now I seem to watch a lot of TV and eat a lot of junk food.
Denise So, what are you gonna do about it?
Ken I'd like to start doing workouts, but I don't know where to start.
Denise You should probably start at the fridge. Throw out your junk food and make sure you've got healthy food to eat.
Ken But I kind of like snacks.
Denise You need to eat better. And get rid of your TV.
Ken What?!
Denise Get serious, get out more often, and get fit.

7 What does Ken want?
8 What did Ken use to do a few years ago?
9 What does Denise suggest?

Go online!

Visit the *Sounds Good* website at *www.sounds-good-online.com*
Click on **Go online!** for extra listening practice.

Online listening

A **3** 25 Listen for key words Two people are being interviewed. Listen and check ☑ the things they do to keep fit and stay healthy.

☐	Walk up and down stairs.	☑	Cut out snacks.
☑	Do some yoga.	☐	Drink green tea.
☑	Lift weights.	☑	Eat healthy food.
☑	Go for walks.	☐	Go dancing.
☐	Go running.	☑	Go swimming.
☑	Do some push-ups.	☑	Play tennis.
☑	Do some sit-ups.	☑	Go cycling.

B **3** 25 Listen for specific information **Listen again and choose the correct answers.**

1 The 70+ Club is for people who ...

 A did not do much exercise when they were young.
 (B) are 70 or over and want to exercise.

2 After they had a great time playing tennis, they decided to ...

 (A) try swimming and yoga.
 B join a fitness club.

3 A few of the 70+ Club members even ...

 A go dancing, and do sit-ups and push-ups.
 (B) do sit-ups and push-ups, and lift weights.

4 After exercise, the 70+ Club members like to eat ...

 A healthy food.
 (B) dessert.

Download *Sounds Good* Podcast 32

Now listen to Podcast 32. You can do the activities, read the transcript, or simpy enjoy listening to young people from around the world.

59

Go online!

Students can visit the *Sounds Good* website at *www.sounds-good-online.com* and click on *Go online!* for extra listening practice based on the unit topic.

Online listening

This section can be used in two ways.

Students can use this for some optional, self-study listening practice outside the classroom. Students will see the same activity as printed in their Student Book and they will be able to complete it online, with immediate feedback on their answer choices.

Alternatively, you can use this section in class as an extension activity. The Online listening is recorded on the Class CDs for this purpose.

Students will listen to a radio interview of Natalie and Walter, two senior people from the Seventy-plus Club.

Audio script [CD3, track 25]

Woman	Hello. Today we are interviewing two very fit people, Natalie and Walter. Now, there are lots of fit people out there, but these two are a bit different … they're both members of the Seventy-plus Club. Natalie, let's begin with you. Tell us what the Seventy-plus Club is all about.
Natalie	Of course, dear. Well, most people think fitness is just for young people. But it's not true. Fitness is a lifetime thing. The Seventy-plus Club is for people seventy or over who keep an interest in exercise and sports.
Woman	Walter, what can you add to that?
Walter	Um, we're not super athletes and a few of us never did much exercise when we were younger, but it's never too late to get started.
Woman	How did the club start?
Natalie	Well, we all used to go to the park in the summer. We sat on benches and chatted, and watched the young people play tennis. Then I suggested that we play tennis with my niece. We had a great time and we decided to do it once a week. Then we started swimming three times a week and then got into yoga. Now a few of us even do some push-ups and sit-ups, and lift weights.
Woman	How many members do you have now?
Natalie	People join the club all the time. Now the club has about sixty members.
Woman	That's great! How about you, Walter? How do you exercise?

Walter	Well, me, I started with walks and swimming, and then I thought I'd try a bicycle. Now I cycle almost everywhere.
Natalie	We also watch what we eat. We try to eat healthy food and cut out the snacks.
Woman	And dessert. I guess neither of you ever eat dessert.
Natalie	I love dessert!
Walter	After all that exercise, we need to eat something sweet!

Podcast 32

Encourage students to download Podcast 32. Inspired by the unit topic, it is authentic and high-interest, and features young people from around the world.

9

Do you ever wear this?

Goals
• Identifying clothing and fashions
• Understanding clothing choices

Learn the language

A **3** **26** **Are fashionable clothes important to you? Match the words and phrases to the pictures. Then listen and number them.**

A	add some highlights	**B**	get a new wardrobe	**C**	in fashion	**D**	comfy
E	pinstripe suit	**F**	striped shirt	**G**	sweatpants	**H**	silver buckle

C 4

B 3

H 7

F 6

A 1

E 2

D 5

G 8

FOCUS

B **3** **27** **Listen and fill in the blanks with the words from the box.**

throw out   new pair   need a makeover   ripped jeans   cry out

1 Why did you _____ *cry out* _____ for fashion help?
   It was actually my sister who thinks I _____ *need a makeover* _____.

2 How long have you had those _____ *ripped jeans* _____?
   For about five years.

3 Why didn't you _____ *throw out* _____ your old sweatpants?
   They're comfy.

4 When's the last time you got a _____ *new pair* _____ of sneakers?
   Two years ago.

60

Unit overview

The topic of this unit is fashion and clothing. In Listening task one, students will listen to two conversations, first between Brian and his sister, then between Brian and Tina, a fashion expert from *Fashion Television*. They are talking about Brian's clothes. In Listening task two, students will listen to four conversations as Brian gets a fashion makeover. In the speaking activities, students will have an opportunity to talk about clothes that they think are in fashion and out of fashion.

Learn the language

- Ask students what the most fashionable clothes are that people are wearing right now. Ask them what sorts of clothes last for a long time and which ones only last for one season.

- Have students open the book and look at the pictures. Ask them what is shown in each picture.

- Read the words and phrases (A–H) and ask students to match them to the pictures.

- Allow students a few minutes to finish writing the answers.

- Review the words and phrases to make sure students understand them all.

- Play the audio (CD3, track 26) and have students number the pictures.

- Review the answers with students by playing the audio again. Stop the CD and play each sentence again as often as necessary.

Language note

Comfy is short for comfortable.
A *wardrobe* can refer to both your clothes and the place where you keep them.

Audio script [CD3, track 26]

1 Add some highlights. Let's add some highlights to your hair.
2 Pinstripe suit. The pinstripe suit looks good.
3 Get a new wardrobe. It's time for me to get a new wardrobe.
4 In fashion. These jeans are in fashion.
5 Comfy. Those old sneakers are comfy.
6 Striped shirt. That striped shirt looks great.
7 Silver buckle. I love this belt with the silver buckle.
8 Sweatpants. These sweatpants look OK.

B

- Have students read through the phrases and sentences to get an idea of what they will be listening for.

- Play the audio (CD3, track 27) and have students fill in the blanks.

- Review the answers by playing the audio again. Check that students understand the expressions.

- Have students role-play the questions and answers in the *Focus* box.

Language note

A *makeover* means changing a person's appearance in several ways, often with a new hairstyle and clothes and, for women, make-up.

Audio script [CD3, track 27]

1

Woman 1	Why did you cry out for fashion help?
Woman 2	It was actually my sister who thinks I need a makeover.

2

Woman	How long have you had those ripped jeans?
Man	For about five years.

3

Woman	Why didn't you throw out your old sweatpants?
Man	They're comfy.

4

Man	When's the last time you got a new pair of sneakers?
Woman	Two years ago.

Listening task one

A **3** **28** Listen for feelings **Brian is talking with his sister. Listen and circle T for True or F for False.**

1 Brian's sister feels excited. Ⓣ　F
2 Brian feels that his clothes are not that bad. Ⓣ　F
3 Brian's sister feels that Brian has nice-looking clothes. T　Ⓕ
4 Brian does not feel surprised at all. T　Ⓕ

B **3** **29** Listen for sequence **Tina, a fashion expert from Fashion TV, is commenting on Brian's clothes. Listen and number the items in the order they are mentioned.**

C **3** **29** Listen for opinions **What does Tina say about Brian's clothing? Listen again and write the name of the item of clothing next to the correct opinion.**

1 It's been quite a few years since that was in fashion. _____suit_____
2 When's the last time you got a new pair? _____sneakers_____
3 It looks kind of old. _____sweatshirt_____
4 Why don't you throw them out? _____sweatpants_____
5 They're three years out of fashion. _____glasses_____

Speak out!

Work with a partner. You have won a fashion makeover with Fashion TV. Tina and her crew are in your home asking you questions. With your partner, role-play the conversation.

Use the language in **FOCUS** to help you.

61

Listening task one

- Introduce the characters, Brian and his sister. Explain that Brian's sister has done a surprising thing.

- Have students read through the statements on the page.

- Play the audio (CD3, track 28) and have students circle T or F.

- Review the answers with students and ask them to summarize what has happened.

Audio script [CD3, track 28]

Sister	Congratulations, Brian. You won!
Brian	Won? What did I win?
Sister	You won a complete makeover with *Fashion Television*. You send in a few pictures of yourself, and a picture of your closet. They pick someone each week to get a new haircut, a new wardrobe and, most importantly, they get rid of your ugly old clothes like those worn-out sneakers and that ugly sweatshirt.
Brian	But … *Fashion Television*, I never heard of it. How could I win anything? I never sent in any pictures.
Sister	Uh, well, no. Actually, I did.
Brian	Really? Why? Are my clothes that bad?
Sister	Yes, Brian. They are.

- Ask students to look at the picture and describe what they see.

- Explain that the woman with sunglasses in the picture is Tina, a fashion expert and the presenter of a fashion makeover show on TV. She is interviewing Brian, a reluctant participant on the show, about his wardrobe. The interview takes place at Brian's house. Students need to number the clothing items in the picture in the order they are mentioned.

- Play the audio (CD3, track 29) and have students number the items.

- Review the answers with students by eliciting the names of the items.

Audio script [CD3, track 29]

Man	OK, ready everyone? Cameras rolling in five, four, three …
Tina	Welcome to another edition of Fashion Disasters. Today we're in the closet of Brian Bean. Brian, welcome to today's show!
Brian	Thanks, Tina.
Tina	Brian, why did you cry out for fashion help?
Brian	Uh, actually my sister sent in the photos.
Tina	And thank goodness she did! Brian, you need help, help, help! Let's start with what you're wearing now. How long have you had your glasses?
Brian	Not so long. About three years.
Tina	They're three years out of fashion. And what about your sweatpants? They're ripped. Why don't you throw them out?
Brian	They're so comfy.
Tina	And your sweatshirt? It looks kind of old.
Brian	Well, I guess so. Maybe a little old.
Tina	And your sneakers. When's the last time you got a new pair?
Brian	Oh, I've had these for years.
Tina	Yes. Just like that suit in your closet. It's been quite a few years since that was in fashion. Does it still fit? And those ties with cartoon characters on them? Don't get me started! Brian, come this way …

C

- Tina has many opinions—most of them rude—about Brian's clothes.

- Have students read through the opinions.

- Play the audio (CD3, track 29) again and have students write the clothing items.

- Put students into pairs and have them decide which opinion is the rudest.

Speak out!

- Review the language in the *Focus* box on the previous Student Book page.

- Put students into pairs and explain that one person is Brian, the other is Tina.

Model conversation

A How long have you had your glasses?

B About three years.

A They're three years out of fashion. And when's the last time you got a new pair of sneakers?

B Oh, years ago.

Unit **9**

Listening task two

A **3** `30-33` [Listen for key details] Brian is getting a fashion makeover. Listen and check ☑ the correct pictures.

1

3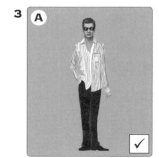

2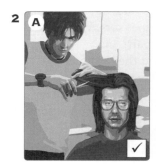

4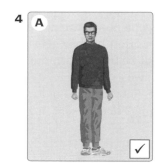

B **3** `30-33` [Listen for specific information] Listen again and circle the correct answers.

1 What item of clothing does Brian want to keep?
  A A jacket with gold buttons.
  (B) A belt with a large gold buckle.
  C A silver jacket.

2 Where does Brian usually get his hair cut?
  A At a salon at the shopping mall.
  B At a small place down the street.
  (C) He cuts it himself.

3 What clothes did Tina choose for Brian?
  A Simple clothes in different colors.
  B Striped shirts and a black jacket.
  (C) Black and white clothes in the latest fashion.

4 Why is Brian's sister surprised?
  A Brian's hair and glasses look great.
  (B) Brian is wearing his old sweatpants and sweatshirt.
  C Brian is wearing clothes he found in the garbage can.

Speak out!

3 `30-33` Listen again and make note of the changes Tina and her crew made to Brian's wardrobe and look. Discuss them with your partner. Do you think these are the right decisions?

Listening task two

- The new language introduced in this section includes the following words, phrases and sentences:

  > Which clothes have you not worn in the last year?
  > giant gold buckle
  > You're a fashion disaster.
  > sunglasses
  > the latest style
  > we saw lots of room for improvement
  > you can mix and match and always be in fashion

- Ask students whether they would like to have a fashion makeover. Why or why not?

- Have students look at the pictures and say what is shown in each picture. What is the difference between each pair of pictures?

- Explain that students will listen to four conversations about Brian's makeover. Point out that the hairdresser in Conversation 2 has a Spanish accent.

- Play the audio (CD3, tracks 30–33) and have students check the correct picture for each conversation.

- Ask students which words and phrases helped them decide the correct picture for each conversation.

Audio script [CD3, tracks 30–33]

1

Man	OK, ready everyone? Closet scene. Cameras rolling in five, four, three …
Tina	Brian! Tell us about your wardrobe. Which clothes have you not worn in the last year?
Brian	Well, I guess … this half.
Tina	Half the clothes in your closet! Well, that's an easy decision. They all have to go.
Brian	Can I keep my old belt?
Tina	The one with the giant gold buckle? Oh, no, no, no. It's already in the trash.
Brian	But, but …
Tina	No buts, Brian. You're a fashion disaster.

2

Man	Hair salon scene. Cameras rolling …
Tina	Now we're at Heroes Hair Salon with Brian Bean. Brian, where do you usually get your hair cut?
Brian	Well, I do it myself—to save money. It's not that hard.
Tina	It's hard to look at. Franco? What can you do with this head of hair?
Franco	Well, first, the shape is wrong and it's too long. We need to add some highlights.

3

Tina	The new hair looks good, but we're not done yet, Brian. Here are your new glasses! And look. New sunglasses, too!
Brian	They look good.
Tina	And I'm sure they feel great. Looking over your wardrobe, we saw lots of room for improvement. We decided to keep it simple. Here we have a black shirt, a white shirt and two striped shirts. These black pants and these jeans go perfectly with them. Everything here is the latest style, so you can mix and match and always be in fashion.

4

Sister	Brian, great hair and I love the glasses, but aren't those your old sweatpants and sweatshirt?
Brian	Uh, yeah.
Sister	But, I thought the TV crew threw them out?
Brian	They did. But they were still in the garbage can. I got them back and my old belt, too.
Sister	I don't believe it!
Brian	Believe it. They're comfy.

- Have students read through the questions and answer choices on the page.

- Play the audio (CD3, tracks 30–33) again and have students circle the correct answers.

- Review the answers with students.

Speak out!

- The aim of this section is to integrate listening with other skills. In this case, students practice note-taking and giving opinions.

- Put students into pairs and explain the speaking activity.

- Play the audio (CD3, tracks 30–33) once more and have students take notes of the changes Tina and her crew made to Brian's wardrobe and look.

- Have students discuss with their partner about the changes and decide whether the changes are the right decisions.

- Ask some pairs to tell the class what they think about the changes.

Model conversation

A I'm glad they cut his hair. It looked too long.
B I'm not sure. I think it was kind of cute.
A Really? But you didn't like his belt, did you?
B I have one just like that!

Write what you hear

A **3** **34** Short words such as *a, in, to, of, out* and *you* often join up with other words. Listen and complete the sentences.

Example: (You won a complete makeover.) ⟶ You ___*won a*___ complete makeover.

1 I never ___*heard of it*___ .

2 Well, that's ___*an easy*___ decision.

3 They're three years ___*out of fashion*___ .

4 It's been ___*quite a few*___ years since that ___*was in fashion*___ .

5 What ___*can you do*___ with this ___*head of hair*___ ?

6 Looking ___*over your*___ wardrobe, we saw ___*lots of room*___ for improvement.

7 ___*You're a fashion*___ disaster.

8 ___*Tell us about your wardrobe.*___

B **3** **34** Now listen again and repeat. Try saying the sentences as naturally as possible.

Use what you learn

A Think about the kinds of clothes that you often see. Make a list of the ones you think are in and out of fashion.

(Answers may vary.)

In fashion	Out of fashion
– skinny jeans	– long skirts
– white belts	– wide ties
– hats	– brown suits
– big scarves	

B Work in groups of three. Ask your group members about the clothes they think are in fashion and out of fashion. Take turns.

A Big belts with silver buckles look good.

B Oh, no. They're out of fashion.

A I don't like striped shorts.

C But they're in fashion now!

A Really?

Write what you hear

Aim

The aim of this section is for students to identify and practice the pronunciation of short words in sentences.

Short words such as *a, in, to, of, out* and *you* are weak words. Most of them are function words which perform certain grammatical functions in sentences. They are not usually stressed and often join up with a strong word.

A consonant at the end of a strong word can link up to a word beginning with a vowel sound:

C+V   *sent+in*   ➔   *'sentin* (link)

A consonant sound at the end of a strong word may blend with or link to a following consonant sound in a weak word:

C+C   *decided+to*   ➔   *decided to* (link)

          about+your   ➔   *aboutchyour* (blend)

- Introduce the topic of short words in sentences and review their definition.

- Point out the example in the exercise and model the sentence.

- Play the audio (CD3, track 34) and have students fill in the missing words.

- Review the answers by playing the audio again. Encourage students to find and correct any of their mistakes.

Audio script [CD3, track 34]

Example: You won a complete makeover.
1 I never heard of it.
2 Well, that's an easy decision.
3 They're three years out of fashion.
4 It's been quite a few years since that was in fashion.
5 What can you do with this head of hair?
6 Looking over your wardrobe, we saw lots of room for improvement.
7 You're a fashion disaster.
8 Tell us about your wardrobe.

- Play the audio (CD3, track 34) again. Have students repeat each sentence out loud, trying to say the sentences as naturally as possible.

- Monitor and provide feedback on students' pronunciation.

Use what you learn

Aim

The aim of this section is to give students the opportunity to talk about the clothes that they think are in fashion and out of fashion.

- Review the unit vocabulary and functional language by asking students what they think the most fashionable clothes and accessories are.

- Have students work individually to make a list of the clothes that they think are in fashion and out of fashion.

- Explain the activity and model the conversation at the bottom of the page with three students.

- Put students into groups of three and have them work together to complete the activity. Encourage groups to talk about clothing items not mentioned in this unit.

Extension

Do a class survey to make a list of the most fashionable clothes.

Unit 9

Your score:

_____ /10

Test yourself

3 **35** You will hear a talk about Tammy's job. You will have to answer ten questions of different kinds. First, read through all the questions. Then listen and answer the questions.

Questions 1–3. Answer the questions below. Choose the correct letter, A, B or C.

1 What do we know about Tammy?

(A) She is a university student and works part-time.

B She works full-time at a clothing store.

C Tammy works part-time as a fashion designer.

2 What do Tammy's parents do?

A They are fashion designers.

(B) They own a clothing store.

C They work at a university.

3 Why does Tammy think her job is different?

A She has to work long hours.

B She doesn't like fashion.

(C) She has to help people find clothes that suit them.

Questions 4–7. Complete the table below. How often do people do different things? Check ☑ the correct answers.

People come into the store …	rarely	occasionally	sometimes	usually
4 just to look around.				✓
5 to look for something special.			✓	
6 and ask for help.	✓			
7 to look for a whole new wardrobe.		✓		

Questions 8 and 9. Complete the sentences below. Use NO MORE THAN THREE WORDS for each answer.

8 Sometimes, what Tammy really wants to say is, _____ *"Get a haircut!"* _____

9 Tammy thinks styles change all the time, but there are things that are _____ *always in fashion* _____.

Question 10. Look at these two sets of notes. Check ☑ the one that best summarizes Tammy's talk.

☐ Tammy works part-time in a store and helps people buy clothes. She enjoys working with customers, especially people who think that some clothes are out of fashion for them.	✓ Tammy works part-time in her parents' store and helps customers find clothes. She enjoys her work, but does not like all of the customers. She finds that some people do not know what is best for them in terms of fashion.

64

Test yourself

Aim

The aim of this section is to provide exam practice. Students will listen to a talk and answer ten questions of different kinds. Explain that the questions are not recorded on the audio.

Explain the test format. Students should read through all the questions and answer choices first to get an idea of what information they need to listen for. While listening to the talk, students may take notes of any key points to help them answer the questions.

When choosing their answers, students need to pay special attention to the wording of the questions, particularly those questions where they are required to use no more than three words for an answer. In questions 8 and 9 where they are required to complete sentences, their answers must also be grammatically correct.

Audio script [CD3, track 35]

Tammy My name is Tammy. Let me tell you a bit about myself and what I do. I'm nineteen years old and a university student. I want to be a fashion designer. Every summer, I work part-time in my parents' store—a clothing store. I like the job because I get to see the latest styles and fashions, but it's not an easy job.

It's not easy because part of what I have to do is help people find clothes that look good on them. The trouble is, most people don't know what looks good on them. Instead, they want to look like someone else … a movie star, someone they saw on TV, even a friend who bought the same clothes. Sometimes this means they want jeans that are too small for them or a shirt that is too big.

Most often, people come into the store just to look around a bit. Sometimes, they might want something special, like an evening dress. People seldom ask me for help; I usually have to ask. And, once in a while, I'll find someone who is looking for a whole new wardrobe. This is usually a guy who has got a new job and needs to look good. I'll help him find a nice suit and a few shirts and maybe a belt. But sometimes, what I really want to say is, "Get a haircut!" Some people need a makeover that is more than just some new clothes.

Most people are really nice, but a few are not. They walk around the store and say, "Oh, this isn't in fashion anymore." It's a silly thing to say. Styles change all the time, but there are things that are always in fashion. Not everyone needs to dress the same.

Go online!

Visit the *Sounds Good* website at **www.sounds-good-online.com**
Click on **Go online!** for extra listening practice.

Online listening

A **3** **36** Listen for implied intention Andy and his friend, Sun-Young, are talking about Andy's clothes. Listen and check ☑ the things that Sun-Young thinks Andy should do.

Throw out your old sweatshirt ☑

Buy some new jeans ☐

Buy a striped shirt ☐

Get a new pair of shoes ☐

Get a haircut ☑

Buy a new suit ☑

Change your glasses ☐

Throw out your old clothes ☑

B **3** **36** Listen for key words Listen again and complete the sentences.

1   So, you need _____*a makeover*_____. Let's start with your hair.

2   And you need a _____*new suit*_____—or two.

3   I'm afraid it's out of fashion—just like that _____*striped shirt*_____!

4   Listen to me, it's really a good time to get rid of _____*your clothes*_____.

5   It's ripped. You should be embarrassed _____*wearing it*_____.

Download *Sounds Good* Podcast 33

Now listen to Podcast 33. You can do the activities, read the transcript, or simpy enjoy listening to young people from around the world.

65

Go online!

Students can visit the *Sounds Good* website at *www.sounds-good-online.com* and click on *Go online!* for extra listening practice based on the unit topic.

Online listening

This section can be used in two ways.

Students can use this for some optional, self-study listening practice outside the classroom. Students will see the same activity as printed in their Student Book and they will be able to complete it online, with immediate feedback on their answer choices.

Alternatively, you can use this section in class as an extension activity. The Online listening is recorded on the Class CDs for this purpose.

Students will listen to a conversation between Sun-Young and her friend Andy, who has just got a new job. Sun-Young thinks Andy needs a makeover. Sun-Young has a Canadian accent.

Audio script [CD3, track 36]

Sun-Young	Congratulations, Andy! I heard you got the new job!
Andy	Yeah, that's right. I start on Monday.
Sun-Young	In that case, it's going to be a busy weekend.
Andy	Busy weekend? What do you mean?
Sun-Young	I mean you have to do something about your clothes.
Andy	What about my clothes?
Sun-Young	You're going to be working in an office, right?
Andy	Right. So?
Sun-Young	So, you need a makeover. Let's start with your hair. How about getting it cut and getting a few highlights?
Andy	Highlights, definitely no. Cut a bit … maybe. But I like it long.
Sun-Young	It's not what you like anymore. It's what the boss likes. And you need a new suit—or two.
Andy	Let's start with one. I can still wear my old suit.
Sun-Young	I'm afraid it's out of fashion—just like that striped shirt!
Andy	You're kidding!
Sun-Young	No, I'm not.
Andy	I just got it … four years ago.
Sun-Young	Listen to me, it's really a good time to get rid of your clothes.

Andy	What are you talking about?
Sun-Young	New job, new life. You need to look good at the office, but you also need to look good in your free time. Take that sweatshirt, for instance.
Andy	It's comfy.
Sun-Young	It's ripped. You should be embarrassed wearing it. Trust me, I'm your best friend.
Andy	You were my best friend. Not any more!
Sun-Young	You'll thank me when you look wonderful at the office and meet the boss's daughter and she marries you.
Andy	Let's just worry about the clothes for now.
Sun-Young	Get your credit card. We're going shopping!

Podcast 33

Encourage students to download Podcast 33. Inspired by the unit topic, it is authentic and high-interest, and features young people from around the world.

Computer Buddies!

Goals
- Identifying computer technology
- Understanding telephone helpline information

Learn the language

A **4 2** How much do you know about computers and the Internet? Match the words to the pictures. Then listen and check your answers.

Internet connection   modem   blog   wireless mouse   cables   password   software

1 *cables*

2 *software*

3 *Internet connection*

4 *password*

5 *blog*

6 *modem*

7 *wireless mouse*

FOCUS

B **4 3** Read about the following computer problems. What do you think is the cause of each problem? Listen and match the problem to the cause.

1	I can't get an Internet connection.	*A*	**A** Your modem isn't working.
2	My hard drive was erased.	*D*	**B** You don't have the right software.
3	I can't seem to get my printer working.	*E*	**C** You don't have enough memory.
4	Someone deleted all my emails.	*F*	**D** You have a virus on your computer.
5	I can't install this new game.	*B*	**E** The printer cable isn't connected to your computer.
6	I can't download this video.	*C*	**F** You have a hacker using your password.
7	Oh no! I deleted your attachment.	*G*	**G** You clicked on the "delete" button by mistake.

68

Unit overview

The topic of this unit is computer technology. In Listening task one, students will listen to a voicemail message at a computer helpline first and then to Patrick, a computer technician, giving advice to people with various computer problems. In Listening task two, students will listen to Patrick telling a story about one caller. In the speaking activities, students will have an opportunity to explain how to use computer applications step by step.

Learn the language

- Ask students what they know about computers and the Internet. Brainstorm some words and phrases on the board.

- Have students open the book and look at the pictures. Ask them what is shown in each picture.

- Read the words in the box and ask students to match them to the pictures.

- Allow students a few minutes to finish writing the answers.

- Review the words to make sure students understand them all.

- Play the audio (CD4, track 2) and have students check their answers. Stop the CD and play each sentence again as often as necessary.

Language note
A *blog* is a web page that contains the information about a particular subject, in which the latest information is usually at the top of the page. Readers can scroll down the page to read earlier news or messages.

Audio script [CD4, track 2]

1 Cables. The cables to my computer are fine.
2 Software. I bought some software for my new computer.
3 Internet connection. I can get a fast Internet connection.
4 Password. No one knows my password.
5 Blog. I've also started my own blog.
6 Modem. I connect to the Internet using a modem.
7 Wireless mouse. I don't use a cable for my wireless mouse.

B

- Explain some of the problems in the *Focus* box to elicit some possible causes from students.

- Have students read through the sentences for problems and causes. Explain that although some problems may have more than one cause, only one cause is spoken on the audio so students cannot simply guess the answers.

- Play the audio (CD4, track 3) and have students match the problems to the causes.

- Have students role-play saying the problems and explaining the causes in the *Focus* box.

Audio script [CD4, track 3]

1
Man 1	I can't get an Internet connection.
Man 2	Your modem isn't working.

2
Woman	My hard drive was erased.
Man	You have a virus on your computer.

3
Man	I can't seem to get my printer working.
Woman	The printer cable isn't connected to your computer.

4
Man 1	Someone deleted all my emails.
Man 2	You have a hacker using your password.

5
Woman	I can't install this new game.
Man	You don't have the right software.

6
Woman 1	I can't download this video.
Woman 2	You don't have enough memory.

7
Woman	Oh no! I deleted your attachment.
Man	You clicked on the "delete" button by mistake.

Listening task one

A 🔵4️⃣ 4 Listen for sequence **Listen to a voicemail message at a computer helpline. Write in the numbers you should press for each service.**

A If you are having problems with your computer, press ___2___.

B If you wish to talk to a technician, press ___4___.

C If you are having problems with your Internet connection, press ___1___.

D If you are having problems with your software, press ___3___.

E If you would like to hear the choices again, press ___5___.

B 🔵4️⃣ 5-8 Listen for key details **Patrick, the computer technician, is giving customers advice on the helpline. Listen and number the pictures to match the conversations.**

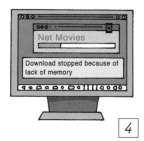

4

1

2

3

C 🔵4️⃣ 5-8 Listen for key words **What advice does Patrick give each person? Listen again and choose the correct sentences.**

PERSON 1

A Make sure your modem is turned on.
B Check the cables are connected.
(C) Try restarting your computer.

PERSON 2

A Use a password that is easy to remember.
(B) Just change your password.
C Do not share your password with strangers.

PERSON 3

A Do not open any attachments.
B Only open attachments from companies.
(C) Don't open attachments if you don't know who they're from.

PERSON 4

(A) Do yourself a favor—just rent the movie.
B Increase your computer's memory.
C Only download short movies.

Speak out!

Work with a partner. Pretend you have one of the computer problems above and you are calling a helpline. Discuss your problem and ask for his or her advice. Take turns.

Use the language in **FOCUS** to help you.

69

Listening task one

- Explain that students will listen to a voicemail message at a computer helpline.

- Have students read through the sentences for the different services.

- Play the audio (CD4, track 4) and have students write the numbers. Review the answers with students.

- Ask students how they feel about voicemail services. Do they find them more or less helpful than speaking to a real person?

Audio script [CD4, track 4]

Woman Thank you for calling Computer Buddies. If you are having problems with your Internet connection, press 1. If you are having problems with your computer, press 2. If you are having problems with your software, press 3. If you wish to talk to a technician, press 4. If you would like to hear the choices again, press 5. Your call is important to us. Please stay on the line until the next available technician is free to help you.

- Patrick, the computer technician, is giving customers advice on the helpline.

- Play the audio (CD4, tracks 5–8) and have students number the pictures. Point out that the man in the fourth conversation has an Australian accent.

- Review the answers with students. What did they hear that helped them decide?

Audio script [CD4, tracks 5–8]

1
Patrick Computer Buddies, thank you for waiting. Patrick speaking.
Man Hi, I'm having problems with my home computer.
Patrick That's what I'm here for. What kind of problems?
Man I can't seem to get a wireless Internet connection.
Patrick Perhaps your modem isn't working. Try restarting your computer.

2
Patrick Computer Buddies, thank you for waiting. Patrick speaking.
Woman Hi, Patrick. I have a blog about my two cats. But someone keeps changing all the pictures to, uh, photos of ugly dogs and putting up stupid messages.

Patrick Mm. On your web log? Sounds like you have a hacker, someone using your password. Have you given your password to anyone?
Woman No, never!
Patrick Well, is your password easy to guess, like the name of one of your cats or something?
Woman How did you know that?!
Patrick Uh … just change your password.

3
Patrick Computer Buddies, thank you for waiting. Patrick speaking.
Man I think I have a virus on my computer.
Patrick What makes you think that?
Man Well, I opened an attachment and the next day I got a message saying my hard drive was erased.
Patrick Do you know who sent the attachment?
Man No, but it said "Important news" on it.
Patrick Don't open attachments if you don't know who they're from. And install software to scan for viruses.

4
Patrick Computer Buddies, Patrick speaking. What can I do for you today?
Man Well, I like to download music and that's no problem, but I keep trying to download this video, and it's just not working. It starts, but it doesn't finish.
Patrick It's like a Hollywood movie?
Man Yeah, it's two hours long.
Patrick Movies take up a lot of memory. Check how much memory you have. If you don't have enough, do yourself a favor—just rent the movie.

C

- Tell the students that they are going to listen for the advice Patrick gives to each person.

- Play the audio (CD4, tracks 5–8) again and have students choose the correct sentences.

- Put students into pairs and have them compare their answers.

Speak out!

- Review the language in the *Focus* box on the previous Student Book page.

- Put students into pairs and explain the speaking activity.

Model conversation

A Computer Buddies, Jack speaking.
B Hi Jack, I can't get an Internet connection.
A Try restarting your computer.

123

Unit **10**

Listening task two

A **4** **9** Listen for gist A man phoned Patrick's computer helpline today. Now Patrick is telling his friend the story. Listen and circle the correct words to summarize Patrick's story.

The man was worried / (upset) because his (email) / modem did not work. Patrick told him (what to do step by step) / to get a new computer .

B **4** **9** Listen for implied purpose What other details can you guess from Patrick's story? Listen again and choose the best answer for each question.

1 Why did Patrick mention that a few callers are very experienced with computers, but some are not?

  A He is suggesting the story is about someone who knows a lot about computers.
  B He is talking in general terms about computers being difficult to use.
  (C) He is suggesting the story is about someone who knows nothing about computers.

2 Why did the man ask Patrick to repeat everything he says?

  A Because he cannot hear very well.
  (B) Because he is writing down Patrick's instructions.
  C Because he is very patient.

3 What did the comment "the screen is all dark" suggest to Patrick?

  A The power has suddenly gone out.
  (B) The man has not plugged his computer in.
  C The computer has been turned off for the day.

4 Why did the man hang up without saying anything?

  A He had spent too long talking to Patrick.
  B He thought Patrick was not helpful.
  (C) He was embarrassed about his foolish mistake.

Speak out!

4 **9** Work with a partner. Listen again and write down the advice that Patrick is giving the man. Pretend you are Patrick and your partner is the person calling. Practice the conversation. Take turns.

1 Have you installed ____ *your email program* ____?

2 ____ *Are your modem cables connected?* ____

3 ____ *What do you see on the screen?* ____

70

Listening task two

- The new language introduced in this section includes the following words, phrases and sentences:

  > very experienced with computers
  > he says he's having a lot of trouble with it
  > "Have you installed your email program?"
  > I tell him how to do it, step by step.
  > "Are your modem cables connected?"
  > screen
  > plug the computer into an electrical outlet

- Ask students what sorts of problems they have with their computers. What do they do when they have a problem? Do they ever call a computer helpline?

- Explain that students will listen to Patrick telling the story of one caller. They need to circle the correct words to complete the summary of Patrick's story.

- Have students read through the summary quickly.

- Play the audio (CD4, track 9) and have students circle the correct words.

- Review the answers with students. What did they hear that helped them decide?

Audio script [CD4, track 9]

Patrick So, let me tell you what happened at work today. You know, I get calls from all sorts of people, and a few of them are very experienced with computers; some are not.

So, today, this man phones up. He's just bought his first computer and he says he's having a lot of trouble with it. I can tell right away that he is very upset. He says it doesn't seem to work at all. First, I ask him,

"What do you want to do with your computer?"
He tells me he wants to use email.
"And what's the particular problem?" I ask.
He says to me, "I don't know how to send messages."

This is not unusual. Email can be a bit confusing the first time, so I'm not surprised. I ask him,
"Have you installed your email program?"
He says, "I don't know how to do that."

So I tell him how to do it, step by step. He listens patiently and asks me to repeat things, several times. I can tell he's writing down my every word. I ask him to try following the

steps, you know, pressing different keys. By now, we've been talking for more than half an hour.

"Did you do everything I asked?"
"Yes," he says. "But it still doesn't work."
I try to imagine the problem and ask him,
"Are your modem cables connected?"
"Yes," he says. "The computer comes with a modem."

After quite a few more questions, I ask him,

"What do you see on the screen?"
"I don't see anything," he says.
"Nothing?"
"No," he says. "The screen is all dark."
"Ah, I understand now. Did you plug the computer into an electrical outlet?"

There's a long pause. He doesn't say anything. Then he just hangs up.

- Have students read through the questions and answer choices to get an idea of what they will be listening for.

- Play the audio (CD4, track 9) again and have students choose the correct answers.

- Have students compare their answers in pairs.

Speak out!

- The aim of this section is to integrate listening with other skills. In this case, students practice note-taking and role-playing a scenario.

- Put students into pairs and explain the speaking activity.

- Play the audio (CD4, track 9) once more and have students write down the advice Patrick gives to the man.

- Play the audio again to give students a chance to check their answers.

- Ask students to role-play the conversation between Patrick and the man.

Model conversation

A Have you installed your email program?
B I don't know how to do that.
A Did you do everything I asked?
B Yes. But it still doesn't work.

Write what you hear

A (4)(10) Short words such as *I, you, your, him, his, her* and *them* are not usually stressed. They are pronounced quickly and quietly, and often join up with other words. Listen and complete the sentences.

Example: What can I do for you today? → What ____*can I*____ do ____*for you*____ today?

1 Try ____*restarting your*____ computer.

2 ____*Just change your*____ password.

3 Have ____*you installed your*____ email program?

4 ____*He's just bought his*____ first computer.

5 I ____*asked him what he*____ wanted to do.

6 And ____*a few of them are*____ very experienced with computers.

7 I try to imagine the problem ____*and ask him*____, "Are ____*your modem cables*____ connected?"

8 First, ____*I ask him*____, "What do ____*you want to do with your*____ computer?"

B (4)(10) Now listen again and repeat. Try saying the sentences as naturally as possible.

Use what you learn

A How do you use your computer? Do you do any of the things listed? Add two more things. _Answers may vary._

Send emails
Send attachments
Watch videos online
Write assignments
Make presentations

B Work in groups of three. Choose one of the things and discuss the steps.

A How do you watch videos online?
B First, you open the website.
A OK.
B Then you search for the video you want to see.
C Then you click on the "play" button.

71

Write what you hear

Aim

The aim of this section is for students to identify and practice the pronunciation of short words in sentences.

> Short words such as *I, you, your, him, his, her* and *them* are not usually stressed. They usually join up with a strong word. When a weak word beginning with the sound /h/ or /ð/ joins up with a strong word, the /h/ or /ð/ sound can disappear. This is most likely to happen when we are speaking quickly, e.g.,
>
> *I asked him* → I ask~~h~~edim
>
> *A few of them* → a few of~~th~~em

A

- Introduce the topic of strong and weak words.
- Point out the example and model the sentence.
- Play the audio (CD4, track 10) and have students fill in the missing words.
- Review the answers by playing the audio again. Encourage students to find and correct any of their mistakes.

Audio script [CD4, track 10]

Example: What can I do for you today?
1 Try restarting your computer.
2 Just change your password.
3 Have you installed your email program?
4 He's just bought his first computer.
5 I asked him what he wanted to do.
6 And a few of them are very experienced with computers.
7 I try to imagine the problem and ask him, "Are your modem cables connected?"
8 First, I ask him, "What do you want to do with your computer?"

B

- Play the audio (CD4, track 10) again. Have students repeat each sentence out loud, trying to say the sentences as naturally as possible.
- Monitor and provide feedback on students' pronunciation.

Use what you learn

Aim

The aim of this section is to give students the opportunity to explain how to use computer applications step by step.

A

- Review the unit vocabulary and functional language by talking about what you use a computer for and asking students what sorts of things they use their computers for. Besides sending emails and surfing the web, answers may include playing games, keeping a calendar and using drawing and photo management programs.
- Have students work individually to add two more things to the list.

B

- Explain the activity and model the sentences at the bottom of the page with three students.
- Put students into groups of three and have them work together to complete the activity. Encourage groups to give clear explanations.

Unit **10**

Test yourself

4 **11** You will hear a lecture. You may take notes while you listen. You will be asked to answer six questions of different kinds. You may use your notes to answer the questions.

1 What would be the best title for this lecture?

   A "Problems I have had with my computer"
   B "Four problems about computers that you should understand"
   C "Hackers and viruses are big computer problems"
   (**D**) "Why people both love and hate their computers"

2 What does the speaker say people do with their computers? Choose TWO answers.

   A Write letters and reports.
   (**B**) Send emails to friends and family.
   C Design posters.
   (**D**) Use them for work.

3 When were the following statements true? Match the statements to the times.

   A No one had their own computer.
   B People cannot live without a computer.
   C Most people need computers.
   D No one had a website.

Time	Event
In the future	*B*
Today	*C*
Twenty years ago	*D*
Forty years ago	*A*

4 The speaker mentions three problems. Put the problems in the order they are mentioned. One problem is extra.

Problem	Order
Cannot open attachments	
Hacker searching for information	*3*
Cannot connect to the Internet	*1*
Virus deletes email	*2*

5 Which of the following does the speaker NOT mention?

   A Many early computer viruses were just small problems.
   B Viruses would show a silly message on your screen.
   (**C**) Friends and family often send viruses by mistake.
   D Viruses often try to erase your hard drive.

6 What does the speaker NOT say about hackers?

   A They go into your computer and take control of it.
   B They search for information, especially information about your bank or credit cards.
   (**C**) They may send emails to your friends to control their computers.
   D They may take or spend all of your money.

10

Test yourself

Aim

The aim of this section is to provide exam practice. Students will listen to a lecture and answer six questions of different kinds.

Explain the test format. Students will have seven seconds after each question to answer the question. Students should read the questions and answer choices first so they have a general idea of the types of information they should listen for. While listening to the lecture, students may take notes of any key points to help them answer the questions.

Point out that the first question requires students to listen for the overall gist of the lecture. In order to choose the best title for this lecture, they need to summarize information from different parts and draw a conclusion about the main topic and purpose of the listening extract.

When choosing their answers, students need to pay special attention to the question types, particularly question 2 where students need to choose more than one answer, question 3 where students are required to match statements to events in a table and question 4 where they need to order information.

Audio script [CD4, track 11]

Man Today's lecture is about how people and computers work together. People both love and hate their computers. They use them at the office for work, but they also use them for sending emails to friends and family. Some people even decorate their computers with stickers or toys. But forty years ago, no one had their own computer. Twenty years ago, there were no web pages. Today, most people need computers. In the future, people will say they cannot live without one. The trouble is, computers are not perfect. That leads to the hate part of working with computers.
Three major computer problems concern people. The first is when people cannot connect to the Internet or send emails. It's often a simple problem that's easy to fix, but it still upsets people. The second problem, which is more serious, is the computer virus. Many early computer viruses were just small problems. They would show a silly message on your screen and tell you to do something to make the message go away. Viruses today are more serious. They often try to erase your hard drive or delete all your emails. Suddenly, your computer is useless. Still, this is not the worst problem. The worst problem is a hacker. A

hacker is someone who goes into your computer and takes control of it. Often, the hacker searches for information, especially information about your bank or credit cards. Soon, you may find that someone is taking or spending all of your money. So what can you do? Buy anti-virus software to protect your computer? But new software does not always work. Choose a new and better password? But other people can find or guess your password. Clearly, we need new ideas.

1   What would be the best title for this lecture?
2   What does the speaker say people do with their computers?
3   When were the following statements true?
4   The speaker mentions three problems. Put the problems in the order they are mentioned.
5   Which of the following does the speaker NOT mention?
6   What does the speaker NOT say about hackers?

Go online!

Visit the *Sounds Good* website at **www.sounds-good-online.com**
Click on **Go online!** for extra listening practice.

Online listening

A **4** **12** Listen for main ideas **Listen to Frances and Simon talking about a computer problem. Circle T for True and F for False.**

1 Frances cannot get an Internet connection.   T (F)
2 Frances thinks she has a hacker.   (T) F
3 Frances got a message from everyone in   T (F)
   her address book.
4 The message read, "I love you."   (T) F
5 Frances should email everyone right away.   T (F)
6 Bob was delighted to receive the message.   (T) F

B **4** **12** Listen for specific information **Listen again and check ☑ the correct answers.**

1 What problem does Simon NOT mention?
   ☐ Not enough memory.
   ☐ Deleted an email.
   ☑ Cannot send attachments.

2 What does Simon think the problem might be?
   ☑ A virus that sends out attachments.
   ☐ A hacker who sends out attachments.
   ☐ A virus that deletes attachments.

3 What should Frances NOT do?
   ☐ Phone everyone on her email list.
   ☑ Send emails to everyone on her email list.
   ☐ Tell everyone about the problem.

10

Download *Sounds Good* Podcast 34

Now listen to Podcast 34. You can do the activities, read the transcript, or simpy enjoy listening to young people from around the world.

73

Go online!

Students can visit the *Sounds Good* website at *www.sounds-good-online.com* and click on *Go online!* for extra listening practice based on the unit topic.

Online listening

This section can be used in two ways.

Students can use this for some optional, self-study listening practice outside the classroom. Students will see the same activity as printed in their Student Book and they will be able to complete it online, with immediate feedback on their answer choices.

Alternatively, you can use this section in class as an extension activity. The Online listening is recorded on the Class CDs for this purpose.

Students will listen to a conversation between Simon and Frances. Frances is having a problem with her computer and Simon is offering advice on what to do about it.

Audio script [CD4, track 12]

Simon	Hey, Frances. You don't look very happy. What's the problem?
Frances	It's my email.
Simon	Well, that's what I'm good at. What can I do for you today? Can't get an Internet connection?
Frances	No, that's fine.
Simon	Not enough memory? Having trouble opening an attachment? Deleted an email?
Frances	No, fine, fine, fine. It's my messages. I think I have a hacker.
Simon	A hacker on your email? That sounds bad. What makes you think that?
Frances	Someone sent a message to all my friends, I mean to everyone in my address book.
Simon	Yes.
Frances	And the message had this line, "I love you!"
Simon	Oh, no!
Frances	It's really embarrassing. I mean, they sent it to my boss and …
Simon	I'm not sure it's a hacker. It might just be a virus, you know what I mean?
Frances	A virus? But my computer is fine …
Simon	I mean like a virus that sends out an attachment.
Frances	Oh, Simon, you have to help me!
Simon	And I will! First, I need to look at your computer, and then—
Frances	But what about all these people? Should I send another email to them telling them about the problem?

Simon	You can talk to them, but don't send an email until I get the virus off your computer. Otherwise, you might just send them another virus.
Frances	Uh … Oh, OK. Uh, but I better start phoning everyone on my email list.
Simon	Are there a lot of people?
Frances	Mm. About a hundred.
Simon	Whew!
Frances	Oh, here's one of them now. Bob! Bob, did you get my email?
Bob	Yes, Frances. I did.
Frances	I want to explain—
Bob	You don't have to, Frances. I love you, too!

 Podcast 34

Encourage students to download Podcast 34. Inspired by the unit topic, it is authentic and high-interest, and features young people from around the world.

11 Seen any good movies?

Goals
- Understanding movie reviews
- Identifying movie terms

Learn the language

A **4 13** Do you like movies? Look at the pictures and decide what kind of movie each one shows. Match the words to the pictures, using the letters A–F. Then listen and write the adjectives under each movie.

A war

B action

C animation

D romance

E horror

F science fiction

imaginative
scary
heartbreaking
amazing
violent
entertaining

amazing

scary

heartbreaking

imaginative

violent

entertaining

FOCUS

B **4 14** Read these comments about different movies. Listen and match the sentences that refer to the same movie.

1 This is a great action movie starring Roland Bates and Anna Mitchell. ___C___

2 This movie tells the story of two teenagers who try to help their sick friend. ___B___

3 This is a terrible comedy with no jokes. The plot turns into a boring car chase. Don't waste your time. ___D___

4 This romance tells a very sad story. It's a real tearjerker. ___A___

A But it ends with a wonderful surprise. I couldn't stop crying.

B I found the movie very realistic. I would recommend it.

C Yes, the two actors both give a great performance.

D Yes, I agree. Even the great performance by Ronny Mills can't hide the poor storyline.

74

Unit overview

The topic of this unit is movies. In Listening task one, students will listen to a movie reviewer talking about four movies. In Listening task two, students will listen to Akiko and Steve talking about the three movies they have seen. In the speaking activities, students will have an opportunity to talk about movies they have seen.

Learn the language

- Ask students what kinds of movies they like to watch. Try to get them to talk about the types of movies, not just the titles of specific movies. Prompt the students with terms like *comedies* and *adventure movies*.

- Have students open the book and look at the pictures. Ask them what kind of movie each picture shows.

- Read the words (A–F) and ask students to match them to the pictures.

- Review the words for movie types. Explain that some movies are combinations of different types, e.g., a science fiction animation.

- Allow students a few minutes to finish writing the answers.

- Read the adjectives in the box and elicit explanations from students to make sure they understand each one.

- Play the audio (CD4, track 13) and have students write the adjectives under the correct picture.

- Review the answers with students by playing the audio again. Stop the CD and play each sentence again as often as necessary.

Audio script [CD4, track 13]

1 Animation. A good animation can be amazing.
2 Horror. I don't like horror movies. They're scary.
3 Romance. A good romance can be heartbreaking.
4 Science fiction. Many science fiction movies are very imaginative.
5 War. Most war movies are too violent.
6 Action. Good action movies are very entertaining.

B

- Review the sentences in the *Focus* box and teach the meaning of new expressions.

- Play the audio (CD4, track 14) and have students match the sentences.

- Review the answers with students by playing the audio again.

- Have students role-play saying the sentences in the *Focus* box as if they were making comments on the movies.

Language note

A movie's *plot* is its story. Another word with the same meaning is *storyline*.

A *tearjerker* is a story that makes you cry.

Audio script [CD4, track 14]

1
Man This is a great action movie starring Roland Bates and Anna Mitchell.
Woman Yes, the two actors both give a great performance.

2
Man This movie tells the story of two teenagers who try to help their sick friend.
Woman I found the movie very realistic. I would recommend it.

3
Woman This is a terrible comedy with no jokes. The plot turns into a boring car chase. Don't waste your time.
Man Yes, I agree. Even the great performance by Ronny Mills can't hide the poor storyline.

4
Woman This romance tells a very sad story. It's a real tearjerker.
Man But it ends with a wonderful surprise. I couldn't stop crying.

Listening task one

A **4** **15-18** Listen for main ideas A reviewer is talking about four new movies. Listen and number them. Then write the name of the movie and circle the correct number of stars to show the reviewer's rating.

Name _____ *Robot World* _____

Name _____ *Gun Shy* _____

Rating

★ — bad
★ ★ — OK
★ ★ ★ — good
★ ★ ★ ★ — great

1

(★ ★) ★ ★

3

(★ ★ ★) ★

Name _____ *Race Across America* _____

Name _____ *First Love, Last Look* _____

2

(★) ★ ★ ★

4

(★ ★ ★ ★)

B **4** **15-18** Listen for opinions Why does the reviewer recommend some of the movies? Why does he *not* recommend others? Listen again and check the correct answers.

1 ☐ not very realistic
   ☑ not very interesting
   ☐ too scary

2 ☑ poor storyline
   ☐ poor performance by the actors
   ☐ too violent

3 ☑ great animation with funny story
   ☐ very imaginative
   ☐ movie just for kids

4 ☑ great performance by the actors
   ☐ interesting characters
   ☐ not much of a tearjerker

Speak out!

Work with a partner. Look at the pictures above and choose a movie you would recommend and a movie you would not recommend. Tell your partner why. Take turns.

Use the language in **FOCUS** to help you.

75

Listening task one

- Explain that students will listen to a movie reviewer talking about four movies on a TV show. They need to number the pictures for the movies in the order they are mentioned. They also have to write down the names of the movies and circle the correct number of stars to show the reviewer's ratings for the movies.

- Have students look at the pictures and say what types of movie each picture shows.

- Play the audio (CD4, tracks 15–18) and have students do the activities.

- Review the answers with students.

- Ask students which words and phrases helped them decide the correct picture for each review and the reviewer's rating for each movie.

Audio script [CD4, tracks 15–18]

1

Man Tonight on *Movie Mix*, we look at four movies opening this week. The first is the science fiction movie, *Robot World*, starring Ronny Clark and Benjamin Westwood. A man wakes after a thousand years to find a world where humans work for robots. The movie tells the story of the violent struggle of humans against machines. Some science fiction fans may like it, but I didn't find the movie very interesting. I wouldn't recommend it.

2

Man The second movie is the comedy *Race Across America*. It's certainly funny—for the first two minutes, but then the plot turns into a boring car chase. Somehow, hundreds of police officers can't catch the two characters, Jerry and Albert, who are both eighty years old! Even the strong performances by Johnny Moore and Roger Lange can't hide the poor storyline. *Race Across America* is a terrible comedy with no laughs. Don't waste your time.

3

Man The third new movie this week is a lot better. The animation *Gun Shy* tells the story of a policeman who is afraid of guns. Everyone thinks he's so tough that he doesn't need to carry one. One day, he picks up a child's toy gun and everything goes wrong. The story is funny, the characters are good and the animation is

excellent. Although it's a kids' movie, I think the whole family will enjoy it.

4

Man The final movie opening this weekend is the best. It's a romance called *First Love, Last Look* starring Jennifer Lee and Mark Croft who both give a great performance. It tells the heartbreaking story of a young man and the woman he loves. She becomes very sick and her boyfriend promises to help her. So, he goes off to medical school to become a doctor. Be prepared, this is a real tearjerker. I couldn't stop crying. But it ends with a wonderful surprise and you'll enjoy it.

B

- Ask students to listen again to find out why the reviewer recommends some of the movies and does not recommend the others.

- Play the audio (CD4, tracks 15–18) again and have students check the correct answers.

- Review the answers with students.

Speak out!

- Review the language in the *Focus* box on the previous Student Book page.

- Put students into pairs and explain the speaking activity.

- Ask some students to tell the class about the movies they would and would not recommend.

Model conversation

A I would recommend *First Love, Last Look*.

B Why?

A It tells a heartbreaking story of a young man and the woman he loves. Jennifer Lee and Mark Croft both give a great performance.

Extension

Have pairs review another movie they have recently seen and share it with the class. Encourage them to use some of the language from this unit.

Unit 11

Listening task two

A **4** **19** Listen for feelings Akiko and Steve are talking about three movies they have seen recently. Which ones did they like, and which ones didn't they like? Listen and check ☑ the correct answers.

	liked	didn't like
Akiko	✓	
Steve		✓

	liked	didn't like
Akiko	✓	
Steve	✓	

	liked	didn't like
Akiko		✓
Steve		✓

B **4** **19** Listen for specific information What is each movie about? Listen again and write the kind of movie each one is. Then check ☑ the correct statement for each movie.

1 Kind of movie _____*horror*_____
  ☑ Two friends explore a lost city they find in a cave.
  ☐ Two friends discover a cave in a lost city they find.

2 Kind of movie _____*action*_____
  ☑ The main character is a very tough guy who saves three teenagers.
  ☐ The main characters are three teenagers who fight bad guys.

3 Kind of movie _____*romantic comedy*_____
  ☐ A crazy professor falls in love with a singer.
  ☑ A rich girl tries to win the love of a crazy professor.

Speak out!

4 **19** Work with a partner. Listen again. Choose a movie and write down what Akiko and Steve like about it, and what they dislike about it. Then think of other movies that are the same kind. Discuss with your partner.

1 Title _____*Cave*_____

2 What they like ____*Akiko – really great horror movie*____

3 What they dislike ____*Steve – terrible, characters were dumb*____

4 Other movies _____*The Ring*_____

76

Listening task two

- The new language introduced in this section includes the following words, phrases and sentences:

  cave
  discover a lost city
  The characters were boring and did dumb things.
  Jeremy Moore played a great character.
  the bomb blew up
  romantic comedies
  It was supposed to be funny.
  Not very believable, I think.

- Ask students about the movies they have seen recently. Which movies did they like? And which ones didn't they like? Ask them to explain why they liked or disliked the movies.

- Have students look at the pictures and say what kind of movie each picture shows.

- Explain that students will listen to Steve and Akiko talking about the three movies they have seen. Students need to find out whether each of them liked the movies or not.

- Play the audio (CD4, track 19) and have students check the correct answers.

- Ask students how Steve and Akiko felt about each movie, e.g., *Akiko liked* Cave, *but Steve didn't.*

Audio script [CD4, track 19]

Steve So, Akiko, have you seen any good movies lately?

Akiko A couple. I went to see a really great horror movie last week.

Steve It wasn't *Cave*, was it? It's about two friends who go into a cave and discover a lost city?

Akiko Yeah, it was excellent. You enjoyed it too?

Steve Not at all. I thought it was terrible. The characters were boring and did dumb things. If you found a lost city, don't you think you would go and tell somebody first?

Akiko No! I'd want to explore first.

Steve Well, it definitely wasn't as good as *The Hunter*. I love that kind of action movie.

Akiko Well, I agree. I loved it too. Jeremy Moore played a great character ... very tough, but realistic.

Steve And funny too! I loved the part where he saved the three teenagers before the bomb blew up.

Akiko Well, maybe that wasn't so realistic. I'm surprised he wasn't killed by the bad guys.

Steve Well, it's a movie, not real life. And all the car chases were good fun.

Akiko Yeah, the chases were really cool, but there was too much shooting, especially at the beginning. Anyway, it's still a lot better than *The Last Kiss*.

Steve Oh, yeah! I saw it just yesterday. What a waste of money!

Akiko I love romantic comedies, but this one was really bad. It was supposed to be funny, but I certainly didn't laugh.

Steve Me, neither. What do you think about the two characters?

Akiko Not very believable, despite the good performances by Tom Lange and Jessica Richards.

Steve Well, the story wasn't very interesting. Why would a rich girl want to win the love of a crazy professor? Not very believable, I think. But I really enjoyed the music.

Akiko Yeah, good songs.

B

- Have students read through the statements.

- Play the audio (CD4, track 19) again and have students write the movie type and check the correct statement for each movie.

- Review the answers with students.

Speak out!

- The aim of this section is to integrate listening with other skills. In this case, students practice note-taking before discussing.

- Put students into pairs and explain the speaking activity. Have pairs choose a movie.

- Play the audio (CD4, track 19) once more and have students write down what Steve and Akiko liked and disliked about the movie.

- Have some pairs tell the class about the movie they chose and the other movies they discussed.

Model conversation

A Akiko liked *The Hunter* because Jeremy Moore played a great character ... very tough, but realistic.

B Steve loved the part where Jeremy saved the three teenagers before the bomb blew up.

A Akiko thought the part where Jeremy Moore saved the three teenagers wasn't so realistic.

B Another great action movie is *The Gun*.

Learn the rhythm

A   **4 20** When we feel enthusiastic, we speak louder and use a higher pitch. When we feel unenthusiastic, we speak more quietly and use a flatter pitch. Listen and add an exclamation mark (!) after the sentences that sound enthusiastic.

Example: I love this kind of action movie.   [!]
I wouldn't recommend it.   [   ]

1   Don't waste your time.   [   ]

2   I think the whole family will enjoy it.   [!]

3   It ends with a wonderful surprise.   [!]

4   I couldn't stop crying.   [!]

5   I went to see a really great horror movie last week.   [!]

6   It was supposed to be funny, but I certainly didn't laugh.   [   ]

7   I loved the part where he saved the three teenagers before the bomb blew up.   [!]

8   Well, the story wasn't very interesting.   [   ]

B   **4 20** Now listen again and repeat. Try saying the sentences marked with an exclamation mark with enthusiastic intonation.

Use what you learn

Answers may vary.

A   Think of a movie you have seen recently. What was it like? Complete the table below.

Title	*The Red Rose*	Storyline	*Young farmer falls in love with a*
Kind of movie	*Romance*		*princess. He grows a new rose and names it*
Actors	*Catherine Wray, Jeff Franklin*		*after her. Dumb movie.*
Opinion	⭐ ★ ★ ★		

B   Work in groups of three. Tell your group about your movie. Ask each other questions. Take turns.

A   I went to see *The Red Rose* this weekend.
B   What kind of movie is it?
A   It's a romance starring Catherine Wray and Jeff Franklin.
C   What's it about?
A   It tells the story of a young farmer who falls in love with a princess.

77

Learn the rhythm

The aim of this section is to distinguish between intonation that expresses enthusiasm and intonation that expresses a lack of enthusiasm. Students will also practice saying the sentences with the appropriate intonation.

> When we feel enthusiastic about what we are talking about, we speak louder and use a higher pitch. The pitch of our voice varies from high to low. However, when we feel unenthusiastic about what we are saying, we speak more quietly and the pitch of our voice is flatter without much variation.

A

- Introduce the topic of intonation and explain how we use pitch to express our attitude about what we say.

- Point out the example and model the two sentences with different intonation. Explain that the pitch fall from high to low is greater on the first sentence than on the second.

- Play the audio (CD4, track 20) and have students add an exclamation mark after the sentences that sound enthusiastic.

- Review the answers by playing the audio again. Encourage students to find and correct any of their mistakes.

Audio script [CD4, track 20]

Example: I love this kind of action movie. [!]
             I wouldn't recommend it.
1 Don't waste your time.
2 I think the whole family will enjoy it. [!]
3 It ends with a wonderful surprise. [!]
4 I couldn't stop crying. [!]
5 I went to see a really great horror movie last week. [!]
6 It was supposed to be funny, but I certainly didn't laugh.
7 I loved the part where he saved the three teenagers before the bomb blew up. [!]
8 Well, the story wasn't very interesting.

B

- Play the audio (CD4, track 20) again. Have students repeat each sentence with the appropriate intonation.

- Monitor and provide feedback on the pitch in students' pronunciation. Focus on the pitch at the end of the sentences.

Use what you learn

The aim of this section is to give students the opportunity to talk about movies they have seen.

A

- Review the unit vocabulary and functional language by discussing a movie you have seen. Elicit comments from students.

- Have students work individually to complete the table.

B

- Explain the activity and model the sentences at the bottom of the page with three students.

- Put students into groups of three and have them work together to complete the activity.

Extension

Ask students to have their own Movie Awards Ceremony. Students will choose several movies and decide if they fit into the categories of action, animation, horror, romance, science fiction or war movies. Students then vote to decide which one is the best in each category. They have to explain what they like and/or dislike about each movie.

Unit 11

Your score:

_____ /14

Test yourself

4 **21** You will hear a discussion in a seminar class. You may take notes while you listen. You will be asked to answer six questions of different kinds. You may use your notes to answer the questions.

1 What is the topic of the discussion?

    A How to create a good movie.
    B How to create convincing characters.
    (C) How to write a good storyline for a successful movie.
    D How to create movie characters.

2 What is the first step in creating a good storyline?

    A Understanding your characters.
    (B) Understanding the different kinds of movies.
    C Learning how to combine features from different movies.
    D Knowing your audience.

3 What are movie genres?

    A Groups of movies starring the same actors.
    B Groups of movies that have the same plot.
    (C) Groups of movies that have similar plots and characters.
    D Groups of characters.

4 What movies do the speakers mention? Number them in the order they are mentioned.

    __4__ A love story combined with the drama of real events and a famous ship.
    __2__ A romantic comedy about a bored princess who falls in love with a reporter.
    __3__ A science fiction movie with characters generated from technology and lots of action.
    __1__ A horror movie about a video that kills everyone who watches it.

5 Which genre is each movie? Check ☑ the genre or genres that each movie is.

	Romance	Romantic comedy	Science fiction	Horror	Action	Drama
The Ring				✓		
Roman Holiday		✓				
Star Wars movies			✓		✓	
Titanic	✓					✓

6 Why do viewers want to know the genre before watching the movie?

    A They want to know the actors.
    B They want to know how long the movie will be.
    C They want to know if it is a good movie.
    (D) They want to know what to expect from the movie.

78

Test yourself

Aim

The aim of this section is to provide exam practice. Students will listen to a discussion and answer six questions of different kinds.

Explain the test format. Students should read the questions and answer choices first so they have a general idea of the types of information they should listen for. While listening to the discussion, students may take notes of any key points to help them answer the questions. When choosing their answers, student need to pay special attention to the question types, particularly question 4 where students are asked to number the movies in the order they are mentioned and question 5 where students are required to match movies to genres in a table.

Point out that Woman 1, the first female student speaking in the discussion, has a Canadian accent.

Audio script [CD4, track 21]

Lecturer	Morning. Today, we're going to talk about how to create a good storyline that can become a successful movie. Any ideas?
Man 1	I think you need to be very imaginative …
Woman 1	And have lots of good ideas.
Man 2	Yes, but it's very important that you understand the different kinds of movies, like dramas, action or horror movies.
Lecturer	That's right. Knowing the different genres is the first step in creating a good story. Movie genres are different groups of movies that have similar plots and characters. Can you give me some examples of movie genres and the stories they tell?
Woman 1	Well, a horror movie usually tells the story of the struggle of a character who tries to defeat a monster, or something supernatural. For example, in the movie *The Ring* people get killed seven days after watching a mysterious video.
Man 2	One of my favorite movies is *Roman Holiday*. It's about a bored princess who falls in love with a reporter in Rome. It's a typical romantic comedy. This genre usually shows someone who tries to win the love of another person.
Lecturer	Good examples. Do you normally find out the kind of movie before you watch it?
Woman 2	Of course, that's how I decide if I want to see it or not.
Lecturer	So, movie genres are important as they tell viewers what to expect from the movie.
Man 2	But most movies usually combine at least two genres.
Lecturer	Yes, that's right. So, if you want to write a good story, you need to know which two genres to combine. For example, a lot of action movies combine some features of science fiction movies. A good example is the *Star Wars* movies where George Lucas combines lots of action with characters generated from technology.
Woman 2	Or *Titanic,* where the love story is combined with the drama of real events and the famous ship.
Lecturer	OK. So we all agree that to turn a good story into a successful movie we need to understand the main genres and how to combine them. Now, for our next study session I would like you to make a list of the basic genres and their features. Thanks a lot, and see you next week.

1 What is the topic of the discussion?
2 What is the first step in creating a good storyline?
3 What are movie genres?
4 What movies do the speakers mention?
5 Which genre is each movie?
6 Why do viewers want to know the genre before watching the movie?

Go online!

Visit the *Sounds Good* website at **www.sounds-good-online.com**
Click on **Go online!** for extra listening practice.

Online listening

A **4 22** Listen for sequence   Carol and Ho-Jin are talking about three movies. Listen and number the posters in the order they talk about them. One poster is extra.

Which movie does Carol want to see? Write the correct number.   1

B **4 22** Listen for key words   What does Ho-Jin say about each movie? Listen again and complete the sentences.

1 It's a _____romantic_____ comedy about two people who rent the same apartment.
The _____characters_____ are not very realistic. The story is not very_____interesting_____.

2 It's a _____horror_____ movie, really _____scary_____.
Let me guess, chickens from space attack the Earth.

3 It's a kind of _____comedy_____ about _____tough_____ cowboys looking for a lost cow.
It's very _____funny_____.

Download *Sounds Good* Podcast 35

Now listen to Podcast 35. You can do the activities, read the transcript, or simpy enjoy listening to young people from around the world.

79

Go online!

Students can visit the *Sounds Good* website at *www.sounds-good-online.com* and click on *Go online!* for extra listening practice based on the unit topic.

Online listening

This section can be used in two ways.

Students can use this for some optional, self-study listening practice outside the classroom. Students will see the same activity as printed in their Student Book and they will be able to complete it online, with immediate feedback on their answer choices.

Alternatively, you can use this section in class as an extension activity. The Online listening is recorded on the Class CDs for this purpose.

Students will listen to a conversation between Ho-Jin and Carol, who are talking about three movies. Carol wants to get advice about which movie she and her friend Maureen should see. Carol has an Australian accent.

Audio script [CD4, track 22]

Ho-Jin	Hello?
Carol	Hi, Ho-Jin. It's Carol. How are you?
Ho-Jin	Fine, Carol, fine. And you?
Carol	Good. I was calling because Maureen and I are going to a movie tonight.
Ho-Jin	Mm-hm.
Carol	And so … you seen any good movies lately?
Ho-Jin	Very funny, Carol. You know I see everything. It's one of the reasons I work at the movie theater.
Carol	Exactly. So, there are three movies at your theater right now …
Ho-Jin	And I've seen them all. Which one are you interested in?
Carol	Don't know. I haven't heard anything about any of them.
Ho-Jin	Well, then. Let's see … There's *Room for One*, a romantic comedy about two people who rent the same apartment. Not funny. Not funny at all.
Carol	No? Why?
Ho-Jin	Oh! Where do I start! The characters aren't very realistic. They all seem too … too nice!
Carol	Well, what happens?
Ho-Jin	The story's not very interesting. Two friends live in a small apartment, then they marry their girlfriends, but none of them want to leave the apartment. I didn't really understand what happened in the end.
Carol	Oh. What else is playing?

Ho-Jin	*Night of the Crazy Chickens*. It's a horror movie, really scary. I loved it.
Carol	Let me guess, chickens from space attack the Earth.
Ho-Jin	How did you know? Anyway, the third one is *Over the Moon*, a kind of comedy and I really liked the characters … tough cowboys looking for a lost cow. It's very funny. I couldn't stop laughing!
Carol	Thanks, Ho-Jin! That's all I need to know.
Ho-Jin	Wait, which one are you going to see?
Carol	The first movie—*Room for One*.
Ho-Jin	But that's the one I said was no good.
Carol	Uh, I hate to say it, but I know that if you don't like a movie, I'll probably love it.

 Podcast 35

Encourage students to download Podcast 35. Inspired by the unit topic, it is authentic and high-interest, and features young people from around the world.

We stick together.

Goals
- Understanding personal qualities
- Identifying feelings

Learn the language

A **4 23** **What do you think makes a good friend? Listen and complete the sentences with the words from the box. Then listen again and check your answers.**

> helps   cheer   crazy   honest   together   sympathy   dreams   trust   forgives   crazes

1 My friend helps me pursue my _____*dreams*_____.

2 We do lots of _____*crazy*_____ things together.

3 My friend is always _____*honest*_____ with me.

4 My friend and I _____*trust*_____ each other.

5 My friend _____*helps*_____ me when I have a problem.

6 My friend and I always stick _____*together*_____.

7 My friend _____*forgives*_____ me if I do something wrong.

8 My friend sends me email jokes to _____*cheer*_____ me up.

9 On tough days, my friend has lots of _____*sympathy*_____ for me.

10 We follow the latest fashion _____*crazes*_____.

B **4 24** **Listen to what these people say about their friends and match the sentences above to the people. Write the numbers 1–10 in the speech bubbles.**

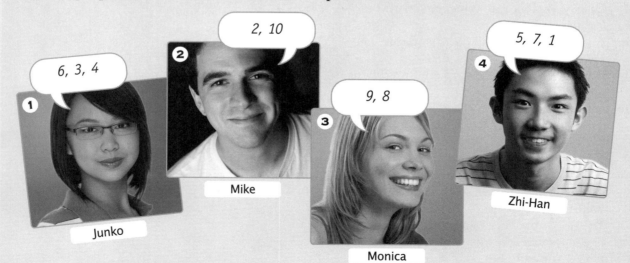

6, 3, 4 — 1 Junko

2, 10 — 2 Mike

9, 8 — 3 Monica

5, 7, 1 — 4 Zhi-Han

80

Unit overview

The topic of this unit is friendship. In Listening task one, students will listen to a song by someone expressing her feelings for a best friend. In Listening task two, students will listen to a song that tells a story about a man named Charlie and his two loves. In the speaking activities, students will have an opportunity to talk about their best friends and the things they do together.

Learn the language

- Ask students what they think the qualities of a good friend are. For each quality, ask students to provide an example.

- Have students open the book and look at Activity A.

- Read the words in the box and ask students to complete the sentences with the words.

- Review the words to make sure students understand what each one means.

- Allow students a few minutes to finish writing the answers.

- Play the audio (CD4, track 23) and have students check their answers. Stop the CD and play each sentence again as often as necessary.

Audio script [CD4, track 23]

1   My friend helps me pursue my dreams.
2   We do lots of crazy things together.
3   My friend is always honest with me.
4   My friend and I trust each other.
5   My friend helps me when I have a problem.
6   My friend and I always stick together.
7   My friend forgives me if I do something wrong.
8   My friend sends me email jokes to cheer me up.
9   On tough days, my friend has lots of sympathy for me.
10 We follow the latest fashion crazes.

B

- Explain that students will listen to four people talking about their friends. They need to match the sentences from Activity A to the four people. Review the names: Junko, Mike, Monica and Zhi-Han. Point out that Junko has a Japanese accent and Zhi-Han has a Chinese accent.

- Play the audio (CD4, track 24) and have students write the numbers of the sentences in the speech bubbles.

- Have students role-play saying the sentences in the speech bubbles as if they were talking about their friends.

Language note

stick together = spend a lot of time in each other's company

Audio script [CD4, track 24]

1
Junko   My name's Junko. My friend and I always stick together. She's always honest with me. We trust each other.

2
Mike   Hi, I'm Mike. I have many friends. We do lots of crazy things together. We follow the latest fashion crazes.

3
Monica   Hi, I'm Monica. I have a very good friend. On tough days, she has lots of sympathy for me. She sends me email jokes to cheer me up.

4
Zhi-Han   My name's Zhi-Han. My friend helps me out when I have a problem. He forgives me if I do something wrong. And he helps me pursue my dreams.

Listening task one

A **4 25** Listen for main ideas **A singer is expressing her feelings for her friend in a song. Listen and check ☑ the sentence that best expresses the main idea of the song.**

1   It is easy to be a good friend during good times.   ☐

2   We are friends because we help each other in different ways.   ☑

3   Your friendship is more important than pursuing my dreams.   ☐

4   There are sometimes dangers to friendships.   ☐

B **4 25** Listen for attitudes **Listen again and circle the best answers.**

1   Why does the singer say her friend brings her sunshine on rainy days?

   A   When the singer is not happy, her friend buys her expensive presents.
   (B)   When the singer is not happy, her friend cheers her up.
   C   On rainy days, they stay at home and dream about sunshine.

2   Why does the singer say, "Your friendship shines through every cloud"?

   A   On cloudy days, they talk about their friendship.
   B   Their friendship makes them proud.
   (C)   Their friendship makes them happy when times are bad.

3   What does the singer's friend do when there are warning signs of looming danger?

   (A)   Her friend makes her understand a possible danger before it happens.
   B   Her friend makes her understand her dreams better.
   C   Her friend emails her jokes to make her happy.

4   What does the singer mean by "You are true"?

   A   She agrees with her friend.
   (B)   She and her friend trust each other.
   C   The singer and her friend have lots of fun.

Speak out!

Work with a partner. What do the singer and her friend do together? Tell your partner. Take turns.

Use the expressions in **Learn the language** to help you.

Listening task one

- Explain that students will listen to a singer singing about her feelings for a best friend. They need to find out the main idea of the song.

- Have students read through the sentences.

- Play the audio (CD4, track 25) and have students check the correct sentence.

- Review the answers with students.

- Ask students which words and phrases helped them decide the main idea of the song.

Language note

Song lyrics differ from spoken language. Lyrics can be more poetic. For example, in conversation you wouldn't say *On rainy days you bring me sunshine*. Instead, you would say *You cheer me up*.

Song lyrics can also be more whimsical or silly. For example, in conversation you wouldn't say *You stick to me like my favorite glue.*, which is a play on words with *stick* and *glue*. Instead, you would say *You're a loyal friend*.

Audio script [CD4, track 25]

On rainy days, you bring me sunshine
Your friendship shines through every cloud
You make every gloomy day seem fine
Pursuing dreams that make us proud

Sending email jokes, following the latest craze
When we're together we laugh so easily
Finding fun in our own special way
My best friend, you're always there for me

My good times are your good times
Your good times are my good times
Our good times are the best of times
When it's us against the world
That's what friends are for

Through the worst and the best of times
I do for you what you do for me
Alerting me to the warning signs
Of looming danger I can't see

My good times are your good times
Your good times are my good times
Our good times are the best of times
When it's us against the world

That's what friends are for

I don't know where I'd be without you
You stick to me just like my favorite glue
Through all of the crazy things we do
You keep my trust, and you are true

On rainy days you bring me sunshine
Your friendship shines through every cloud
You make every gloomy day seem fine
Pursuing dreams that make us proud

My good times are your good times
Your good times are my good times
Our good times are the best of times
When it's us against the world
That's what friends are for

My good times are your good times
Your good times are my good times
Our good times are the best of times
When it's us against the world
That's what friends are for

- Have students read through the four questions and answer choices.

- Play the audio (CD4, track 25) again and have students circle the best answers.

- Review the answers with students.

Speak out!

- Review the expressions in *Learn the language* on the previous Student Book page.

- Put students into pairs and explain the speaking activity.

- Have some pairs tell the class what the singer and her friend do together.

Model conversation

A The singer and her friend pursue their dreams together.
B They do lots of crazy things together.

Extension

Have pairs think of other good things about a best friend and write another verse for the song.

Unit **12**

Listening task two

A **4** **26** Listen for sequence A singer is telling the story of Charlie and his two loves. Listen and number the pictures.

Then one day their world fell to pieces.

Bernadette saw him walking across the room.

When Charlie saw Angelina, he knew he couldn't resist her beauty.

Bernadette asked him to stick around.

B **4** **26** Listen for attitudes Listen again and circle the best answers.

1 Bernadette wondered, "Am I dreaming or is this real?" because …

   A she had just woken up.
   (B) she thought she and Charlie were in love.
   C she was watching TV and felt very tired.

2 "Two strangers wiped their tears" means in the end …

   A they cried for love.
   B they were sad to get together again.
   (C) they were sad because they were no longer together.

3 Charlie could not believe his luck because …

   (A) he felt Bernadette was everything he wanted.
   B Bernadette did not know about Angelina.
   C Angelina and Bernadette were friends.

4 The emails from Madrid probably upset Bernadette because …

   (A) she found out about Charlie's other girlfriend.
   B all of the emails were written in Spanish.
   C none of the emails were for Bernadette.

Speak out!

4 **26** Work with a partner. Listen again and take notes. Try telling the story to your partner. What do you think will happen to Charlie next? Discuss with your partner.

12

82

Listening task two

- The new language introduced in this section includes the following phrases and sentences:

  he knew he couldn't resist
  reached out for each other
  Two strangers wiped their tears and said goodbye
  stick around
  couldn't believe his luck
  their world fell to pieces

- Ask students what love stories they know. What is the storyline? Discuss the concept of a love triangle. This has been the premise for love stories throughout history.

- Have students look at the pictures and read through the captions for the pictures. Ask them to say what the people are doing in each picture.

- Explain that students will listen to the song *Two Strangers* about Charlie and the two women he falls in love with.

- Play the audio (CD4, track 26) and have students number the pictures.

- Review the answers with students.

Audio script [CD4, track 26]

When Charlie saw her, he knew he couldn't resist
The light that shone from her eyes
And when Bernadette saw him walking across the room
She wondered, am I dreaming or is this real?

Two strangers in a crowd, reached out for each other
Two people looking for someone to hold and kiss
Two lovers in the night, under a moonlit sky
Two strangers wiped their tears and said goodbye

So Bernadette asked him to stick around
And soon the days turned into months
And Charlie just couldn't believe his luck
She was everything that he could hope for

Two strangers in a crowd, reached out for each other
Two people looking for someone to hold and kiss
Two lovers in the night, under a moonlit sky
Two strangers wiped their tears and said goodbye

Then one day their world fell to pieces
Bernadette found the emails from Madrid
Charlie just couldn't believe it was over
But Bernadette could never forgive

Two strangers in a crowd, reached out for each other
Two people looking for someone to hold and kiss
Two lovers in the night, under a moonlit sky
Two strangers wiped their tears and said goodbye

When Charlie saw her, he knew he couldn't resist
The light that shone from her eyes
And when Angelina saw him walking across the room
She wondered, am I dreaming or is this real?

- Ask students to read through the questions and answer choices.

- Play the audio (CD4, track 26) again and have students circle the best answers.

- Review the answers with students.

Speak out!

- The aim of this section is to integrate listening with other skills. In this case, students practice note-taking and then retelling a story.

- Put students into pairs and explain the speaking activity.

- Play the audio (CD4, track 26) once more and have students take notes.

- Have students take turns telling part of the story to their partners and then discuss what they think will happen to Charlie next.

- Ask some pairs to tell the class the story and what they think will happen to Charlie.

Model conversation

A What do you think will happen to Charlie next?
B I'm not sure. He's not very nice.
A Do you think he'll be happy with Angelina?
B Some people never change. I think Charlie will go on meeting new women and upsetting his old girlfriends.

Write what you hear

A **4 27** Rhyming words are often used at the end of song lines. Listen to two parts of the song and fill in the missing lyrics, including the rhyming words.

On rainy days, you (1) _____ *bring me sunshine* _____.

Your friendship shines through (2) _____ *every cloud* _____.

You make every gloomy day (3) _____ *seem fine* _____.

Pursuing dreams that make (4) _____ *us proud* _____.

I don't know where I'd (5) _____ *be without you* _____.

You stick to me just like my (6) _____ *favorite glue* _____.

Through all of the (7) _____ *crazy things we do* _____.

You keep my trust, and (8) _____ *you are true* _____.

B **4 27** Now listen again and repeat. Try singing along and listen out for the rhyming words.

Use what you learn

A What makes a good friend? What are the things that you look for in your friends? What things do you do with your friends? Fill in the chart with examples. | Answers may vary. |

I look for friends who …	My friends and I …
– I can trust	– stick together
– are fun	– do crazy things
– help me with my	– help each other
problems	– have fun together
– make me laugh	

B Work in small groups. Tell your group members about your best friend and the things you do together. Take turns.

A Who is your best friend?
B His name's Hiroshi.
C What makes him special?
B I can always trust him.
D What do you do together?
B We do lots of crazy things together.

Write what you hear

Aim

The aim of this section is for students to identify the rhyming words in song lyrics. Students also sing the lyrics to practice the rhythm and timing of words and syllables.

The lyrics, or words, of a song are organized into lines, and these in turn are organized into groups of lines called verses. In most songs, the word at the end of one line in a verse sounds like the word at the end of another line in the same verse. This is called a rhyme. And the two words with similar sounds are called rhyming words. The rhyming words share the same vowel sound and any following consonant sounds, e.g., _sunshine_ and _fine_, _cloud_ and _proud_. Sometimes, other sounds in the pair of rhyming words sound alike, e.g., the /l/ and /r/ sounds in _cloud_ and _proud_.

Rhyming words are strong words. The strong words in a song fall on the strong beats and sound louder and longer. The weak beats are sung more quietly and quickly.

The pattern of rhyming words at the end of lines, together with the alternating pattern of strong and weak words, or beats, in each line give each song its uniqueness.

A

- Introduce the topic of rhyming words in song lyrics. Explain about lyrics, lines, verses in a song and the definition of a _rhyme_.

- Demonstrate a rhyme with a pair of rhyming words, e.g., _true_ and _you_, _green_ and _clean_. Point out that the vowel sound and any following consonants in the words are the same.

- Play the audio (CD4, track 27) and have students fill in the missing words.

- Review the answers by playing the audio again. Ask students to underline the rhyming words in the song lyrics. Encourage them to find and correct any of their mistakes.

Audio script [CD4, track 27]

On rainy days, you bring me sunshine
Your friendship shines through every cloud
You make every gloomy day seem fine
Pursuing dreams that make us proud

I don't know where I'd be without you
You stick to me just like my favorite glue
Through all of the crazy things we do
You keep my trust, and you are true

B

- Play the audio (CD4, track 27) again. Ask students to sing along and listen out for the rhyming words.

- Monitor and provide feedback on students' performance.

Extension

Choose a popular English song. Play the song for the students and ask them to write down the lyrics and then underline any rhyming words.

Use what you learn

Aim

The aim of this section is to give students an opportunity to talk about their best friend and the things they do together.

A

- Review the unit vocabulary and functional language by asking students about their good friends and the things they do together.

- Have students work individually to fill in the chart with examples.

B

- Explain the activity and model the sentences at the bottom of the page with four students.

- Put students into small groups and have them work together to complete the activity.

- Have some students tell the class about their best friend and the things they do together.

Your score:

_____ /9

Test yourself

4 (28) **You will hear three short talks. You will be asked to answer three questions about each talk. Choose the best response to each question.**

1 Who is the speaker's best friend?

   A Her cousin.
   B Her classmate.
   (C) Her brother.
   D Her father.

2 What do they like to do as they get older?

   (A) Stick together.
   B Get together with family.
   C Trust other people.
   D Talk to each other.

3 Why does the speaker's friend have a lot of sympathy for her?

   A She got a new job at a big company.
   (B) He knows how hard some things are for her.
   C He wants to take her out for dinner.
   D He feels better when they are together.

4 What is the speaker talking about?

   A Having sympathy for old friends.
   B Making friends with people who share your dreams.
   C Making new friends.
   (D) Saying goodbye to a good friend.

5 What is one way the speaker showed his sympathy?

   (A) He helped Peter with his homework.
   B He helped Peter become a doctor.
   C He made sure Peter got into college.
   D He helped Peter pursue his dream.

6 What is the big difference between the speaker and Peter?

   A Peter had a dream of playing professional sports.
   B Peter wanted to go to college.
   C The speaker didn't like watching movies.
   (D) Peter and the speaker did not share the same dream.

7 What is the speaker talking about?

   A The type of friend she cannot trust.
   (B) The qualities of a good friend.
   C How some friends share bad news.
   D Why you cannot keep some friends.

8 What does the speaker say makes a really good friend?

   (A) A good friend is someone you can trust.
   B A good friend is true to your old friends.
   C A good friend shares your bad news.
   D A good friend shares your good news.

9 Why does the speaker say it is important to forgive friends?

   A Only some people are perfect friends.
   B You want to share bad news with old friends.
   C It is hard to make new friends.
   (D) When you find a good friend you want to keep him or her.

12

Test yourself

Aim

The aim of this section is to provide exam practice. Students will listen to three short talks, each followed by three questions, and choose the correct answer to each question from four answer choices.

Explain the test format. Students will have seven seconds after each question to choose the correct answer. Students should read the questions and answer choices first so they can have an idea of what specific information they should listen for.

Audio script [CD4, track 28]

Questions 1 through 3 refer to the following talk.

Woman　I've known my best friend my whole life. He's my brother! Of course, life hasn't always been perfect. Sometimes, we get into fights. Sometimes, we don't want to talk to each other. But, as we get older, more and more we like to stick together. He has a girlfriend and I have a boyfriend and sometimes we do things together. It's fun. My brother is always honest with me and he knows how hard some things are for me so he has a lot of sympathy when things go wrong. Last year, I tried to get a job at this big company. I didn't and my brother was there to take me out for dinner and cheer me up. He's a great friend and a great brother.

1　Who is the speaker's best friend?
2　What do they like to do as they get older?
3　Why does the speaker's friend have a lot of sympathy for her?

Questions 4 through 6 refer to the following talk.

Man　There comes a time when some of us have to say goodbye to a good friend. It's never easy but, in my case, it was the best thing to do. My friend Peter and I always liked the same things and always did lots of crazy things when we were young. But there was one big difference between us. I was good at school and he wasn't. Of course, I had a lot of sympathy and I worked with him on his homework as much as I could. But Peter didn't always think it was important. In his free time, he wanted to play sports or go to the movies instead. But I had a dream of going to college and becoming a doctor. I wanted to pursue that dream and it meant doing a lot more work at school and studying evenings and weekends. Peter didn't understand. It wasn't his dream.

4　What is the speaker talking about?
5　What is one way the speaker showed his sympathy?
6　What is the big difference between the speaker and Peter?

Questions 7 through 9 refer to the following talk.

Woman　I have a pretty good idea about what makes a good friend. The first thing you want in a friend is for that person to always be honest. This means you have someone you can trust. For example, you know that when you tell that person something, they won't go and tell everyone else. Of course, you can tell any friend your good news. Last year, for example, I started seeing a new guy. At the time, I felt I wanted everyone to know. But, it didn't last. When it was over, I was really sad and felt terrible. You only want to share that kind of bad news with a really good friend. Of course, sometimes people make mistakes. Nobody is perfect! That's why I think it's important that you can forgive a friend. It's hard to find a really good friend. When you have one, you want to keep him or her.

7　What is the speaker talking about?
8　What does the speaker say makes a really good friend?
9　Why does the speaker say it is important to forgive friends?

Go online!

Visit the *Sounds Good* website at **www.sounds-good-online.com**
Click on **Go online!** for extra listening practice.

Online listening

A **4** **29** Listen for specific information Listen to two friends talking about a trip. Which place are they talking about? Check ☑ the correct picture.

A  ☐

B  ☑

C  ☐

Will Lee take Pat on the trip? Check ☑ the correct answer.

Yes ☐ No ☑

B **4** **29** Listen for opinions Listen again and check ☑ the answers to show what Pat and Lee think is important in a friend.

A good friend is someone who …	Pat	Lee
does lots of crazy things.	✓	☐
alerts you to danger.	☐	✓
has lots of sympathy.	✓	✓
sticks with you.	✓	☐
is always true.	☐	✓
pursues the same dreams as you.	✓	☐
forgives you.	✓	✓

12

 Download *Sounds Good* Podcast 36

Now listen to Podcast 36. You can do the activities, read the transcript, or simpy enjoy listening to young people from around the world.

85

Go online!

Students can visit the *Sounds Good* website at *www.sounds-good-online.com* and click on *Go online!* for extra listening practice based on the unit topic.

Online listening

This section can be used in two ways.

Students can use this for some optional, self-study listening practice outside the classroom. Students will see the same activity as printed in their Student Book and they will be able to complete it online, with immediate feedback on their answer choices.

Alternatively, you can use this section in class as an extension activity. The Online listening is recorded on the Class CDs for this purpose.

Students will listen to a conversation between Pat and Lee. Lee is going on a trip to France that he won. Pat wants to go with him. Lee has a Canadian accent.

Audio script [CD4, track 29]

Pat   Hey, Lee! How are you doing?

Lee   Great. Really great.

Pat   I guess so! I heard you won the trip to France. It's a trip for two, isn't it?

Lee   Yes, I was meaning to tell you.

Pat   You were? Really? It does sound exciting. A trip to France … two weeks … all expenses paid. And for two. Wow.

Lee   It's really difficult to decide who to take with me.

Pat   Uh-huh. You probably want to take a friend who does lots of crazy things—like me.

Lee   Oh, I don't know … I don't like friends who do lots of crazy things.

Pat   You don't?

Lee   No, crazy things can be dangerous. I'd rather have a friend who alerts me to danger! It's important to have a friend who has lots of sympathy.

Pat   Oh, I agree. I think friends who have lots of sympathy are important, too. Hey, remember when you were in the hospital last year? That was terrible.

Lee   Yeah, but … you never came to see me.

Pat   But I thought about you a lot. It's important to have friends who stick together.

Lee   Mm. It's important to have friends who are always true.

Pat   Oh, is that like pursuing the same dream? You know, it's always been a dream of mine to go to France.

Lee   Well, that's what I wanted to talk to you about. That and the money you took out of my wallet last month.

Pat   You're not still mad about that, are you? I told you I was just borrowing it.

Lee   Yes, and I think it's important to have a friend who can forgive you.

Pat   I couldn't agree more! Forgiving friends is very important.

Lee   So, I hope you'll forgive me for taking someone else to France with me.

 Podcast 36

Encourage students to download Podcast 36. Inspired by the unit topic, it is authentic and high-interest, and features young people from around the world.

Review Test 1

Review Test 1

A 🎧 **37** **You will hear a conversation. You may take notes while you listen. You will be asked to answer six questions about different kinds. You may use your notes to answer the questions.**

Your score ____ /13

1 Who already knows each other? Choose two responses.
- Ⓐ Yuji and Jason.
- Ⓑ Jason and Maria.
- Ⓒ Maria and Yuji.
- D Maria and her Spanish teacher.

2 Where does Maria come from?
- Ⓐ A place north of Madrid.
- B A place south of Madrid.
- C Toledo.
- D Madrid.

3 What languages do Jason and Maria speak? Check ☑ the languages for each speaker.

Languages	Maria	Jason
Arabic		✓
French	✓	
Spanish	✓	✓
German		

4 Which of the following details are found in the discussion? Choose two responses.
- Ⓐ Maria's time in Spain.
- Ⓑ Where Maria is from.
- Ⓒ Yuji's time in Toledo.
- Ⓓ A place Jason visited.

5 Why did Jason go to Avila? Choose two responses.
- Ⓐ To go to a festival.
- Ⓑ Because he took the wrong train.
- C To see Maria.
- D To go to university.

6 What do the speakers NOT talk about? Choose two responses.
- A The languages they speak.
- Ⓑ Their families.
- C The places they come from.
- D The things they like doing.

B 🎧 **38** **You will hear ten questions, each followed by three responses. They are not printed in your book. Choose the best response to each question.**

Your score ____ /10

1 Ⓐ B C
2 A Ⓑ C
3 Ⓐ B C
4 A B Ⓒ
5 Ⓐ B C
6 A Ⓑ C
7 A B Ⓒ
8 A Ⓑ C
9 A Ⓑ C
10 A B Ⓒ

Your score ____ /6

C 🎧 **39** **You will hear two short talks. You will be asked to answer three questions about each talk. Choose the best response to each question.**

1 What two languages is Klaus studying?
- A English and Italian.
- B German and Italian.
- C English and German.
- D French and Italian.

2 What does Klaus say is great about the university?
- A The students.
- B The teachers.
- Ⓒ The library.
- D The lake.

3 What does Klaus say is the worst thing about Konstanz?
- Ⓐ It's hard to find a café in the summer.
- Ⓑ There aren't enough tourists in the summer.
- C There are too many cafés.
- D There are too many tourists in the winter.

4 Where did the speaker find the survey?
- A In a library.
- B In a newspaper.
- C On a TV show.
- Ⓓ In a magazine.

5 What does the speaker say was the one reason kids liked snow?
- A They could see their friends at school.
- Ⓑ They could make snowmen.
- C They could make snowmen at school.
- D It made the Christmas trees pretty.

6 What does the speaker say are the two things that everyone loved?
- Ⓐ Christmas trees and presents.
- B Christmas trees and snow.
- C Presents and decorating Christmas trees.
- D Snow and seeing family and friends.

D 🎧 **40** **You will hear a short talk. Write the missing words.**

Your score ____ /6

Dictation

I read (1) ___this survey___ in a magazine the other day about what people like (2) ___about Christmas___. It was quite interesting because people liked and disliked (3) ___different things___ for different reasons. Take snow, for example. Young kids all (4) ___loved snow___ because they could (5) ___make snowmen___ and also it sometimes meant that they (6) ___didn't have to___ go to school.

Total score ____ /35

Review Test 2

A

36 You will hear a conversation about Eric's job. You will have to answer six questions of different kinds. First, read through all the questions. Then listen and answer the questions.

Your score ___ /8

Questions 1 and 2. Answer the questions below. Choose the correct letter, A, B or C.

1 What is the toughest part of Eric's job?

A He doesn't like to fly.
B He hates the food on the airplane.
(C) He works long hours.

2 Which of the following are difficult for Eric?

A Traveling to other countries.
B Having friends come to stay.
(C) Having plants and pets.

Question 3. Answer the question below. Choose THREE letters A–F.

3 Which of the following does Eric mention?

(A) Visas.
B Passengers.
C Arrival cards.
(D) Passports.
E Food on the airplane.
(F) Free tickets.

Questions 4 and 5. Answer the questions below. Write NO MORE THAN TWO WORDS for each answer.

4 Why does Eric like his job?
He thinks it's great to be able to go to ___different countries___.

5 Who does Eric think he should marry?
He thinks he should marry another ___flight attendant___.

Question 6. Read the two paragraphs and check ☑ the one that best summarizes the conversations.

✓ Eric is talking to a student who is writing an article for a student newspaper. She is asking about his job as a flight attendant and he talks about the good and bad parts of it.

☐ Eric is talking to a reporter who is writing an article for a city newspaper. She is asking about the good and bad things that are part of his job as a flight attendant.

B

37 You will hear two conversations. You will be asked to answer three questions about what the speakers say in each conversation. Choose the best response to each question.

Your score ___ /6

1 Which chore does the woman NOT mention?

A Vacuuming and mopping the floors.
(B) Hanging up her clothes.
C Walking the dog.
D Cleaning her room.

2 Where did the woman go on Tuesday night?

A A play.
(B) A football game.
C A movie.
D To hear a new band.

3 Why is the man asking if she is going to work on Saturday night?

A He wants to get tickets for a comedy show.
B He wants to go clubbing.
(C) He booked tickets for a comedy show.
D He bought tickets for a magic show.

4 Where is the conversation taking place?

A At the check-in desk.
(B) In an airplane.
C At an airport.
D At the information desk.

5 What is the woman missing?

A Her purse.
B Her tickets.
(C) Her briefcase.
D Her backpack.

6 Who had the missing item?

A The woman, under her seat.
B The flight attendant, on another seat.
C The flight attendant, in an overhead compartment.
(D) Another passenger, at his seat.

C

38 You will hear a short conversation. Write the missing words.

Your score ___ /6

Dictation

A What do you (1) ___want to___ do this weekend?
B Nothing. I'm afraid I've got (2) ___chores to do___.
A Chores? You (3) ___can't be___ busy all weekend.
B I'm afraid so. I need to vacuum and mop the floors, (4) ___water the plants___, walk the dog, clean my room. ...
A OK, OK. I get it. But why (5) ___didn't you do___ your chores during the week?
B Well, (6) ___I've been out___ every night.

Total score ___ /20

Review Test 3

A [3 37] You will hear ten questions or statements, followed by three responses. They are not printed in your book. Choose the best response to each question or statement.

Your score /10

1 A B C
2 (A) B C
3 A (B) C
4 A B C
5 A (B) C
6 A B C
7 A (B) C
8 A B C
9 (A) B C
10 A B C

B [3 38] You will hear two short conversations. You will be asked to answer three questions about each conversation. Choose the best response to each question.

Your score /6

1 What did Robert say didn't fit anymore?
A His suits and T-shirts.
B His belts and pants.
(C) His jeans and T-shirts.
D His coat and hat.

2 What days does Robert go to the fitness club?
A Sunday, Tuesday and Friday.
B Monday, Wednesday and Friday.
(C) Monday, Wednesday and Saturday.
D Saturday, Wednesday and Friday.

3 What problem did Robert have?
A He put on weight even though he joined the fitness club.
(B) He lost so much weight, he needed new clothes.
C He didn't have enough clothes for work.
D He couldn't get a new job after he lost weight.

4 What does Miranda say she wants to do for dinner?
A Eat something healthy in front of the TV.
B Make pizza at home.
C Make pizza at home with healthy ingredients.
(D) Eat something healthy.

5 What does Wei-Zhong say he wants to do for dinner?
A Stay home and order a pizza.
(B) Walk to the shopping mall and eat at a restaurant.
C Order pizza from a restaurant at the shopping mall.
D Drive to the shopping mall to have pizza.

6 Why does Miranda want to order pizza?
A She doesn't want to eat in a restaurant.
B She doesn't want to drive.
(C) She doesn't want to walk.
D She doesn't want to go shopping afterwards.

C [3 39] You will hear a talk about Isabella's lifestyle and job. You will have to answer six questions of different kinds. First, read through all the questions. Then listen and answer the questions.

Your score /7

Question 1. Answer the question below. Choose TWO letters A–F.

1 Which of the following foods does Isabella mention?
A Pizza.
B Fried rice.
C French fries.
D Hot dogs.
E Barbecued ribs.
F Fried chicken.

Questions 2 and 3. Answer the questions below. Choose the correct answer, A, B or C.

2 What does Isabella say about her clothes?
A They started feeling comfy again.
B They were too small.
C They weren't fashionable any longer.

3 Why does Isabella say, "I didn't need to be asked twice"?
A She was not sure about it.
(B) She really wanted to teach the class.
C She had taught a fitness class before.

Questions 4 to 6. Complete the sentences below. Use NO MORE THAN THREE WORDS for each answer.

4 Isabella started off _lifting some weights_ and tried a yoga class.
5 One day _the fitness instructor_ was sick and she taught the class.
6 She enjoyed it and the manager offered _her the job_ .

D [3 40] You will hear a short conversation. Write the missing words.

Your score /6

Dictation

A What (1) _do you feel_ like for dinner, Miranda?
B I don't know. Maybe (2) _something healthy_ .
A How about some pizza?
B Pizza isn't healthy, is it?
A Oh, it can be healthy. It's mostly (3) _about portion control_ —how much you eat.
B OK. What (4) _kind of pizza_ do you want to order?
A Oh, I thought we'd (5) _go out for dinner_ . Let's try the new pizza restaurant (6) _in the shopping mall_ .

Total score /29

Review Test 4

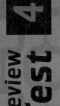

A [4][30] **You will hear a lecture. You may take notes while you listen. You will be asked to answer six questions of different kinds. You may use your notes to answer the questions.**

Your score ___ /9

1 What is the main topic of the lecture?
A Different ways we can watch TV.
B The availability of free music and movies on the Internet.
C Computers are vital for many jobs.
(D) The Internet is changing the way we interact with each other.

2 What does the speaker say people can easily find?
A Hundreds of movies on TV.
(B) Endless amounts of information.
C Many radio stations on the Internet.
D Movie theaters in every neighborhood.

3 What are some of the points that the speaker makes? Check ☑ the statements that are mentioned.

☑ Many people get to know others on the Internet.
☐ Some people on the Internet can be dangerous.
☑ One of the areas in which computers are really changing the way people behave is entertainment.
☐ People should stop using their computers for entertainment.
☑ Before television, people used to get together in the evening, and talk or read together.

4 Which of the following ideas are found in the discussion? Choose two answers.
(A) People sit alone at their computers and don't share their feelings with others.
B Computers are likely to be replaced with new entertainment systems.
(C) The computer has become the new TV and the new stereo system.
D No one would have thought the computer would become so important for entertainment.

5 What comparison does the speaker make between computers and MP3 players?
(A) Now people use computers and MP3 players to listen to music on their own.
B Now people use computers and MP3 players to listen to music together.
C People listen to music with friends and family.
D MP3 players and computers are good for sharing music.

6 What does the speaker mean when she says, "We need to find a way to use computers to share entertainment with friends and family."?
A People should only be alone with their computers for work and watch television with friends.
B People should turn off the TV and get out more to lead a healthier life.
(C) Entertainment is something that is best shared with friends and family, not done alone.
D When you listen to music, you should share it with other people.

B [4][31] **You will hear two short talks. You will be asked to answer three questions about what the speakers say in each talk. Choose the best response to each question.**

Your score ___ /6

1 What do a lot of people NOT know?
A They don't know how much movies cost.
(B) They don't know very much about downloading movies.
C They don't know how to get free movies from the Internet.
D They don't know how much you have to pay to download a movie.

2 What is the speaker's first point?
(A) Movies are not free.
B You can give away your own movies.
C Movies only cost money at movie theaters and video stores.
D Movies are always free on the Internet.

3 What is the speaker's second point?
A It takes a short time to download a movie.
B Most movies are too long to download.
(C) It takes a long time to download a movie.
D Short movies only take a week to download.

4 How does the speaker say actors change on the screen?
A They can get taller and shorter.
B They can turn into aliens.
(C) They can get older and younger.
D They can look mean or cheerful.

5 What does the speaker suggest will be the future of movies?
A Actors will not have the same qualities.
B Everything will be made by computer.
C Anyone can be a moviemaker.
(D) Actors will exist only on hard drives.

6 Why does the speaker suggest moviemakers might be happy in the future?
(A) They won't have to pay actors.
B Everyone will make movies.
C Computers will make movies.
D Actors will make their own movies.

C [4][32] **You will hear a short talk. Write the missing words.**

Dictation

Good afternoon. (1) _This week_ I continue this series of lectures on the impact of the Internet. Everyone agrees that the (2) _Internet has changed_ the way many of us (3) _live our lives_. All of a sudden, people (4) _can easily find_ to find enormous amounts of information that they (5) _had never been able_ before. But the Internet is also changing (6) _the way we interact_ with one another.

Total score ___ /21

Review tests audio script

Review Test 1

Audio script [CD1, track 37]

Maria [Spanish accent]:
Hi, Yuji. Mind if I join you?

Yuji Oh, hi Maria. No, not at all. You know Jason?

Maria No. Hello, Jason.

Jason Hi. You're the new student in our biology class?

Yuji Yeah, Maria just came from Spain.

Maria That's right.

Jason Whereabouts? I mean, whereabouts in Spain are you from?

Maria Ah, a small place, just north of Madrid.

Jason What's the name?

Yuji Isn't it Avalon or something?

Maria Avila. Have you heard of it?

Jason Well, yes. I have. I went there three years ago. I was in Madrid on my way to Toledo, to go to a festival.

Maria But Toledo is south of Madrid, not north.

Jason I know, I know … I took the wrong train. So, you speak Spanish and English and … ?

Maria And French. How about you? Do you speak Spanish?

Jason Yeah, I do. And some Arabic.

1   Who already knows each other?
2   Where does Maria come from?
3   What languages do Jason and Maria speak?
4   Which of the following details are found in the discussion?
5   Why did Jason go to Avila?
6   What do the speakers NOT talk about?

Audio script [CD1, track 38]

1   Have you always lived in Japan?
    A No, I grew up in Spain.
    B No, I grew up in a village.
    C Yes, I'm from Russia.

2   Anything you don't like about Christmas?
    A I like the snow.
    B I don't like the weather.
    C I love getting presents.

3   Where do you come from?
    A [Russian accent] I come from Russia.
    B I speak Russian and English.
    C I came here yesterday.

4   What did you do last night?
    A I'm going to make a snowman.
    B There's a party tonight.
    C I put decorations on the Christmas tree.

5   You're from New York, aren't you?
    A No, I'm from Los Angeles.
    B There are three students from Los Angeles.
    C Los Angeles is in California.

6   What's something you like about New York?
    A I don't like the noise.
    B I like the different restaurants.
    C New York is in the United States.

7   What's the best part of Christmas?
    A I like fall best.
    B The best part of fall is going back to school.
    C The best part of Christmas is seeing Santa Claus.

8   Excuse me, do you mind if I join you?
    A No, I don't speak French.
    B No, not at all.
    C No, I'm not.

9   What part of the country are you from?
    A I grew up in Spain.
    B I'm from New Orleans, in the south.
    C I'm from England.

10   Anything you don't like about the city?
    A Yes, I grew up in the city.
    B Yes, I like everything.
    C I really don't like the pollution.

Audio script [CD1, track 39]

Questions 1 through 3 refer to the following talk.

Klaus [German accent]:
Hi, my name's Klaus and I come from a small town in the south of Germany, called Konstanz. Konstanz is a beautiful place on a lake—Lake Konstanz. Konstanz also has a very nice university. I'm a student at the university and I study French and Italian. The best thing about the university is the library. It has over two million books and it's open twenty-four hours a day. The worst thing about Konstanz? Let me think … I guess it's the tourists. In the summer, it's hard to find a café that's not full of tourists. But, generally, it's a great place to live.

1   What two languages is Klaus studying?
2   What does Klaus say is great about the university?

3 What does Klaus say is the worst thing about Konstanz?

Questions 4 through 6 refer to the following talk.

Woman I read this survey in a magazine the other day about what people like about Christmas. It was quite interesting because people liked and disliked different things for different reasons. Take snow, for example. Young kids all loved snow because they could make snowmen and also it sometimes meant that they didn't have to go to school. But a lot of older people thought snow was one of the worst parts of Christmas because it made it dangerous to drive. Everyone loved Christmas trees and, of course, almost everyone loved decorating their Christmas trees. As you might guess, everyone loved presents too, although some parents said that it was expensive to buy so many presents. But the thing that everyone liked best was seeing friends and family.

4 Where did the speaker find the survey?
5 What does the speaker say was the one reason kids liked snow?
6 What does the speaker say are the two things that everyone loved?

Audio script [CD1, track 40]

Woman I read this survey in a magazine the other day about what people like about Christmas. It was quite interesting because people liked and disliked different things for different reasons. Take snow, for example. Young kids all loved snow because they could make snowmen and also it sometimes meant that they didn't have to go to school.

Review Test 2

Audio script [CD2, track 36]

Woman Hi Eric, I'm doing an article on jobs for my student newspaper. Can you answer a few questions about being a flight attendant?
Eric Of course. Ask anything you want.
Woman Thanks. Let's start with this: What's the toughest part of your job?
Eric Oh, I don't know. It's the long hours, I guess. I have to be at the airport early—well before the airplane takes off. But there are lots of other things I love about the job.
Woman Like what?

Eric Well, traveling, of course. It's great to be able to go to different countries as part of your job, but I also like to travel on my own. I can get free tickets so that's great.
Woman But it must be expensive to stay in hotels.
Eric Some countries are cheaper than others. And, after a while, you make lots of friends and sometimes stay at their places. It's not so expensive. And, of course, they come visit me.
Woman You must go through a lot of passports.
Eric That's right, I do. I get a lot of visas and stamps in my passport, so it fills up fast. I need a new passport every year or so.
Woman What other problems are there?
Eric Well, I can't have a cat or a dog—I'm just away too often. Even if I go away for one night, who's going to walk and feed the dog?
Woman And plants? You can't have plants either?
Eric No, I'm away too often for too long, often a week or more. I don't have anyone who can water them.
Woman So, I guess it would be tough to get married too.
Eric Oh, not at all. I just need to marry another flight attendant.

Audio script [CD2, track 37]

Questions 1 through 3 refer to the following conversation.
Man What do you want to do this weekend?
Woman Nothing. I'm afraid I've got chores to do.
Man Chores? You can't be busy all weekend.
Woman I'm afraid so. I need to vacuum and mop the floors, water the plants, walk the dog, clean my room—
Man OK, OK. I get it. But why didn't you do your chores during the week?
Woman Well, I've been out every night.
Man Every night?
Woman Yeah, Monday I went to a play. Tuesday night was a football game. Wednesday night I saw a movie. Thursday I went to hear a new band.
Man And tonight?
Woman Tonight I'm going clubbing. So, that just leaves Saturday and Sunday to do all my chores.
Man But you're not going to work Saturday night, are you? I booked tickets online for a comedy show.
Woman Sorry. I think I'll be too tired.

1 Which chore does the woman NOT mention?
2 Where did the woman go on Tuesday night?
3 Why is the man asking if she is going to work on Saturday night?

Review tests audio script

Questions 4 through 6 refer to the following conversation.

Woman Excuse me.

Man 1 Yes, can I help you?

Woman It's my briefcase. I put it in the overhead compartment.

Man 1 Oh, is it this one here? This black one?

Woman No, it's not. I mean, it's black, but that's not mine.

Man 1 Well, I'm sure it's here somewhere. It's not under your seat?

Woman No, and I have everything in it. My passport, my money, my computer …

Man 1 It must be here somewhere. It can't have left the plane!

Woman I don't think it's funny and—there, that man there—he's got my briefcase!

Man 1 Excuse me, sir. Is that your briefcase you're looking at?

Man 2 Oh, did I pick up the wrong one? Sorry about that. Here you are.

Man 1 Everything OK?

Woman Mm … let's see … my computer's here, passport … where's my wallet?!

Man 2 Oops! Must have fallen out when I opened it.

4 Where is the conversation taking place?

5 What is the woman missing?

6 Who had the missing item?

Audio script [CD2, track 38]

Man What do you want to do this weekend?

Woman Nothing. I'm afraid I've got chores to do.

Man Chores? You can't be busy all weekend.

Woman I'm afraid so. I need to vacuum and mop the floors, water the plants, walk the dog, clean my room—

Man OK, OK. I get it. But why didn't you do your chores during the week?

Woman Well, I've been out every night.

Review Test 3

Audio script [CD3, track 37]

1 How long have you had this black suit?
   - A I have two black suits.
   - B My suit is black with thin white stripes.
   - C I've had it for three years.

2 When's the last time you bought a new pair of shoes?
   - A I bought some just a few days ago.
   - B I like that hat with stripes on it.
   - C I can't remember. A belt with a big buckle, I suppose.

3 We're invited to a potluck dinner tomorrow.
   - A OK, let's order several dishes to share.
   - B OK, we can bring some tacos to share.
   - C I hope it's not in an expensive restaurant.

4 Do you do yoga in the fitness club?
   - A No, I already had lunch, thanks.
   - B No, but I lift weights three times a week.
   - C They're my favorite band.

5 What did you do to your hair?
   - A I bought a new hat.
   - B I added some highlights.
   - C I'm wearing a new T-shirt.

6 How does she keep in great shape?
   - A She joined a fitness club, but doesn't go there very often.
   - B She hates working out at the fitness club.
   - C She goes to a fitness club five times a week.

7 What's your favorite kind of healthy food?
   - A I really like coffee and chocolate.
   - B Salad and green tea, I guess.
   - C The café is right around the corner.

8 Do you ride your bicycle often?
   - A No, I never use my car if I don't have to.
   - B No, I have two bicycles.
   - C Yes, I never use my car if I don't have to.

9 Why don't you throw out those ripped jeans?
   - A They're still in fashion.
   - B No, I want to keep my belt with the silver buckle.
   - C No, they're not so comfortable.

10 Do you want to grab a cappuccino?
   - A That's the name of the café.
   - B No, I never eat it.
   - C No, thanks. I prefer green tea.

Audio script [CD3, track 38]

Questions 1 through 3 refer to the following conversation.

Robert Hi, Andrea.

Andrea Hey, Robert. You look great! Is that a new suit?

Robert Yeah, just got it.

Andrea Did you start a new job or something?

Robert No, same old job, new suit.

Andrea Well, it looks good … you look good. You working out these days?

Robert Yeah. I was trying to lose some weight. My old jeans and T-shirts didn't fit anymore. So I started eating smaller portions and also joined a fitness club. Now I go Mondays,

Wednesdays and Saturdays for about two hours each time. I used to drive there, but now I walk or run.

Andrea That's great. And now you can fit into your old clothes!

Robert Actually, no.

Andrea No?

Robert No, I'm afraid I lost too much weight. Now my old clothes are too big.

Andrea Really?

Robert Don't laugh! It cost me a lot of money to buy a new wardrobe!

1 What did Robert say didn't fit any more?
2 What days does Robert go to the fitness club?
3 What problem did Robert have?

Questions 4 through 6 refer to the following conversation.

Wei-Zhong What do you feel like for dinner, Miranda?

Miranda I don't know. Maybe something healthy.

Wei-Zhong How about some pizza?

Miranda Pizza isn't healthy, is it?

Wei-Zhong Oh, it can be healthy. It's mostly about portion control—how much you eat.

Miranda OK. what kind of pizza do you want to order?

Wei-Zhong Oh, I thought we'd go out for dinner. Let's try the new pizza restaurant in the shopping mall.

Miranda Sounds good.

Wei-Zhong OK. Let's walk there.

Miranda You don't want to drive?

Wei-Zhong You were the one who wanted to get healthy … let's get some exercise before dinner.

Miranda Maybe you can walk, Wei-Zhong, and I … I can take the car.

Wei-Zhong No way! Come on, don't be lazy.

Miranda Or maybe we should order pizza.

Wei-Zhong Miranda, this is the problem. You want to be healthy, but you don't want to work at it.

4 What does Miranda say she wants to do for dinner?
5 What does Wei-Zhong say he wants to do for dinner?
6 Why does Miranda want to order pizza?

Audio script [CD3, track 39]

Isabella My name is Isabella Harding and I'm a fitness instructor. Fitness is one of the most important things in my life. I work out as part of my job, five days a week, so I don't have to worry about doing any other exercise, but it hasn't always been this way. Five years ago, I had a weight problem. I didn't like my clothes. I

needed a lot more than a makeover. I needed a new life. So, like so many other people, I joined a fitness club. But, unlike so many other people, I didn't quit after a few weeks. I started off lifting some weights. The weightlifting really made me stronger but I wasn't losing weight. Next, I tried a yoga class. I started to lose some weight and, of course, I stopped eating junk food … you know, no more big plates of fried rice and barbequed ribs. I started eating healthy food and felt better. My clothes started to feel comfy again, so I was really happy about that as well.

One day, I went to the fitness class and there was a problem. The instructor wasn't there—she was sick. But there were thirty people waiting. "Hey, Isabella," someone said. "You can teach the class, can't you?" I didn't need to be asked twice. I taught the class and I enjoyed it. After, the manager thanked me and said I was really good. "If I'm so good," I said, "Maybe you'd like to give me a job." Well, that's how I became a fitness instructor!

Audio script [CD3, track 40]

Wei-Zhong What do you feel like for dinner, Miranda?

Miranda I don't know. Maybe something healthy.

Wei-Zhong How about some pizza?

Miranda Pizza isn't healthy, is it?

Wei-Zhong Oh, it can be healthy. It's mostly about portion control—how much you eat.

Miranda OK. what kind of pizza do you want to order?

Wei-Zhong Oh, I thought we'd go out for dinner. Let's try the new pizza restaurant in the shopping mall.

Review Test 4

Audio script [CD4, track 30]

Woman Good afternoon. This week I continue this series of lectures on the impact of the Internet. Everyone agrees that the Internet has changed the way many of us live our lives. All of a sudden, people can easily find enormous amounts of information that they had never been able to find before. But the Internet is also changing the way we interact with one another. For example, many get to know people online and spend time with them instead of getting to know people in real life. People can also buy things online without leaving their homes. But one of the areas in which the

Internet is really changing the way people behave is entertainment. The computer has become the new TV and music system. People download music and television and movie programs—or parts of them. Instead of watching an entire one or two hour show, people can look at video websites that have a few minutes of the so-called best parts. One problem is that people are spending more and more time at their computer alone. Before television, people used to get together in the evening and talk or read together. When television arrived, people still sat around it and laughed at a good comedy or were scared together at a good horror movie. But now? People sit alone at their computers and don't share their feelings with others. The same is true of music. People download songs onto MP3 players and listen to the music on their own. We need to find a way to use computers to share entertainment with friends and family.

1 What is the main topic of the lecture?
2 What does the speaker say people can easily find?
3 What are some of the points that the speaker makes?
4 Which of the following ideas are found in the discussion?
5 What comparison does the speaker make between computers and MP3 players?
6 What does the speaker mean when she says, "We need to find a way to use computers to share entertainment with friends and family."?

Audio script [CD4, track 31]

Questions 1 through 3 refer to the following talk.

Man A lot of people don't understand very much about downloading movies from the Internet. They think they have found an easy way to get new movies for free. They're wrong. They're very wrong. First of all, movies are not free. No one gives them away for free—except people who don't own them. That means you're doing something against the law. Second, it can take a long time to download a movie; your computer might have to work for a week to download a movie. Then, where are you going to put it? A movie takes up a lot of space on your hard drive. Maybe you put it on a DVD—but you also have to worry about viruses. It's a lot of time and work to download a movie and one virus can destroy your computer. I know. I lost my computer that way.

1 What do a lot of people NOT know?
2 What is the speaker's first point?
3 What is the speaker's second point?

Questions 4 through 6 refer to the following talk.

Woman The computer has made enormous changes to the way movies are made. Many filmmakers now use special effects. They can use computers to change what we can see, meaning that there is no limit to what a movie can be about. Almost any special effects are now possible using computer graphics. Background objects can be drawn on a computer and then mixed with live action. Life-like dinosaurs can walk again and aliens can invade Earth from distant stars. The characters we see on the screen can change, too. They can be made to look older or younger. Some actors are even in the computer—they only exist on the hard drive. But they are so realistic we sometimes cannot tell the difference between a real person and a computer-generated image. Already, people have tried making movies where there are no human actors. So far, it's difficult for these actors to show the same qualities as real people, but that will soon change. People who watch movies may not care and the people who make movies will be very happy. And movie makers will never have to pay their actors!

4 How does the speaker say actors change on the screen?
5 What does the speaker suggest will be the future of movies?
6 Why does the speaker suggest moviemakers might be happy in the future?

Audio script [CD4, track 32]

Woman Good afternoon. This week I continue this series of lectures on the impact of the Internet. Everyone agrees that the Internet has changed the way many of us live our lives. All of a sudden, people can easily find enormous amount of information that they had never been able to find before. But the Internet is also changing the way we interact with one another.

Great teachers inspire

Great teachers motivate

Great teachers change the world